SHATTERED TO Shining

JOURNEYS OF SURVIVING AND THRIVING AFTER DOMESTIC VIOLENCE

STORIES OF STRENGTH AND SUCCESS

Compiled by KC Andrews

Copyright © Broken to Brilliant™

The moral right of the authors has been asserted.

First published in Australia in 2019
by Broken to Brilliant Ltd™, Brisbane, Australia
www.brokentobrilliant.org

ISBN

Paperback: 978-0-9945714-5-8

Epub: 978-0-6486540-0-1

Mobi: 978-0-6486540-1-8

Audiobook: 978-0-6486540-2-5

All rights reserved. No part of this book may be reproduced or transmitted by any person or entity (including Google, Amazon or similar organisations), in any form or by any means, electronic or mechanical, including photocopying, recording, scanning or by any information storage and retrieval system, without prior permission in writing from the publisher.

Publishing Consultant/Managing Editor: Belinda Pollard
Copyediting/proofreading: Alix Kwan, Annette Lawson
Cover images copyright © Solarseven, Maridav, FinaLee via Bigstock.com

A catalogue record for this book is available from the National Library of Australia

PRAISE FOR *SHATTERED TO SHINING*

WHAT STICKS WITH YOU IN WORKING in the field of domestic violence is the isolation women feel in these relationships as they constantly struggle to reconcile the positive feelings they have for their partner and the slow loss of self, being dragged under by his manipulation, abuse, intimidation and violence. They can just feel so alone and ashamed.

Shattered to Shining is an important read for anyone interested in understanding more about domestic violence, especially if they have concerns in their own relationships, or wish to learn how others have overcome abuse. It offers easy-to-read case studies about individuals who have lived with abuse and its resultant fallout. Brilliantly it provides individualised positive checklists at the end of each survivor story that could become turning points for other survivors, to help them move on and create a new and richer life away from their abuser.

The lived experience of survivors is an important touchpoint especially for other survivors struggling to understand what is happening to them, and to provide hope that things can change and life can get better. It does not hide from the reality that the struggle can be long and difficult, and each story starts with the individual survivor's bravery to begin the process of reconnecting with their true self.

The stories will also provide assistance and guidance to friends and family to better their understanding of the impact

of domestic violence on their loved one, and to service providers who may use these in a therapeutic setting or to improve their own understanding. The book provides easy to read information about red flags of abuse, referral agencies and other relevant information about how to move forward.
Angela Lynch AM, CEO, Women's Legal Service Qld

RAW, HONEST, COMPELLING – YOU WILL not be able to read these stories without being touched by the amazing resilience and inner strength of each contributor. Real stories that don't gloss over the hard issues, that confront and inspire the reader to look again at situations and to bring hope and see the opportunities to rebuild.

Such a wonderful compendium of practical steps, ideas and strategies make this publication a powerful resource for those faced with domestic abuse in all its ugly forms as well as those who provide support.

You can read one person's account at a time, but I suspect if you are like me, you will not be able to put this book down. I commend it to you and congratulate each and every person on their candid content, reflections and encouragement given.

These are incredible stories that need to be told as a lesson for us all and so that people can see that there is a roadmap for the journey to a much brighter destination. *Shattered to Shining* provides that roadmap.
Bruce Argyle, Head of Philanthropy, Community Sector Banking

THE NARRATIVES FOUND IN *SHATTERED TO Shining* which tell us about journeys of strength, as survivors of domestic violence rebuild their lives after surviving years of incredible abuse. I can think of nothing more terrifying than finding your home, the place where you hope to find comfort, safety and love, is actually the place where physical and sexual violence, emotional and psychological control dominate your every waking moment on a daily basis.

This book allows us to hear the stories of those who found the courage to walk away and start a new life where violence, dominance and control played no part. Many of the relationships started out with hope and love, their partners were charming and manipulative at the beginning of the relationship, however, trust and love was quickly replaced with cruelty and terror.

The stories are authentic, honest, powerful and personal, they are open and frank about the challenges and barriers they faced as well as dealing with their own emotional vulnerability. However, it is because of such honesty that the book will provide hope and solace to many others who are unsure whether they can find the courage and strength to leave an abusive relationship and start to rebuild their life.

This book also helps us to understand why they often felt powerless to leave the relationship. Leaving and rebuilding a new life was not easy for most, and each individual found the inspiration and strength required to build their new lives in different ways. However, what is consistent in every single story is the immense courage it took to actually take that first step. Each person rebuilt their self-esteem, self-worth and wellbeing in different ways. For some it was exercise, nutrition and mindfulness. For others it was study, friends, family and church. Escaping the violence was often dangerous and protracted for some and others had many obstacles put in their way, but nevertheless, they all found the courage and strength to escape.

Thank you to all the contributors to this text. Your willingness to share your story is a testament to your absolute bravery and generosity of spirit. Your deep exposure of your feelings and experiences deeply touched me just as I am sure it will touch every reader. I hope it reaches those who need to read it the most – those who are currently experiencing domestic violence. I sincerely hope they can gain strength and hope from your story.
Dr Kathleen Baird, Associate Professor, School of Nursing and Midwifery – Griffith University, Director of Education, Women, Newborn & Children's Services – Gold Coast University Hospital

'I UNDERSTAND THAT I AM NOT unlovable.' Very powerful words from one of the authors in *Shattered to Shining*. They are words that resonate on every page as these brave people share their painful stories but also their positive conclusions.

I am so privileged to have been invited into their lives through their very honest and personal words. I felt like I was holding my breath as I shared the emotion these authors must have experienced as they went back to a time they'd rather forget.

This is more than just a book, it's an essential resource for those going through domestic violence who feel there is nowhere to turn, but also for those of us who have lived a fortunate life, one not bruised by emotional, psychological and physical violence.

Shattered to Shining will leave you shocked at what these authors have been through but then proud of the strength they've shown to escape and thrive. I applaud the Broken to Brilliant team for also including the story of a male survivor of domestic violence. Though fewer in number, there are men in our community also struggling.

To think these authors have all selflessly shared their trauma to help others is truly inspiring.

Congratulations to all. Continue to thrive.
Loretta Ryan, Breakfast co-host, ABC radio Brisbane

I HAVE JUST FINISHED READING A preview copy of *Shattered to Shining*. I am pausing now before I type my next words as I try to digest the enormity of what I have just read. This book has been quite a journey for me as I am sure it will be for all of those who read it.

I read these stories, firstly, through the eyes of a mental health nurse who has worked in various mental health settings, including hospital inpatient wards, urban communities, forensic units, prisons, overseas detention centres, remote Indigenous communities, hospital emergency departments, and people's homes. In all the locations where I have worked I have seen the endless stream of consequences of domestic violence. Secondly, I read these stories as a person who has had the lived experience of domestic/family violence during my teenage years.

The previously unspoken epidemic of domestic violence is

slowing, thankfully, becoming an issue that people, governments, and organisations are more and more willing to face, discuss, and deal with. Dedicated organisations such as Broken to Brilliant need to be given enormous credit for the education of the public at large regarding just what domestic violence is, and how widespread it is, whilst simultaneously supporting the victim/survivors of this devastating scourge on our society.

The stories included in this book *Shattered to Shining* (written by eleven women and one man), are honest, disturbing, amazing, shocking, inspiring and very real. All of the authors have struggled desperately in their lives through domestic violence on numerous levels including psychologically, emotionally, financially, physically, spiritually, sexually and every way imaginable. The way that these people (and their children in many cases), have endured and survived their torturous circumstances is indeed praiseworthy, but the way that they have risen above their situation and come out the other side with such positivity, strength, commitment and empathy for others, is quite miraculous.

We thank these amazing people for their telling of their stories as they will inspire and give hope to many other people in the years, and I suspect decades, to come.

Huge thanks must also go to the Broken to Brilliant team for the incredibly professional, insightful and nurturing manner in which they have assisted and supported the authors to find their voices in such an honest and impactful way. Congratulations… well done!

Trevor Galbraith, Registered Nurse, Credentialed Mental Health Nurse, Brisbane, Australia

As with the other Broken to Brilliant books, I am amazed at the bravery and determination shown by the authors of *Shattered to Shining*. The benefit of other survivors reading these stories is incredible. Knowing they are not alone and sharing their recovery journey is very powerful. This book is an insightful, well written tool for others. It encourages resilience and shows that positive outcomes do happen. Well done, guys.
Kelly Chamberlain, Branch Manager, Queensland Police-Citizens Youth Welfare Association

This is not just another book.

It is shattered victims' voices heard.

It is shining survivors' stories of strength and success shared.

May each word you read allow the brave, resilient and brilliant you to emerge.

With each page turned may it guide you to a new chapter in your life.

THANK YOU

To each author, thank you for being brave, resilient and brilliant in sharing your story.

The authors of *Shattered to Shining* have shared over 50,000 heartfelt words that leap from the pages with a range of emotions. Bringing each word to life means an immersion into forgotten pain, remembering the abuse that was suppressed, feeling the shame, betrayal and rejection all over again. The key step for our authors is to feel and acknowledge the pain without staying stuck or wallowing in it.

Each of these authors has reflected, and celebrated how far they have come. They have given many hours to developing their chapters, without fame or financial gain. They have shared their story of feeling shattered and the steps they took to be their shining selves, in order to help you move forward on your journey after abuse. They want to help you and 'pay it forward' to another survivor.

To Community Sector Banking, thank you for your financial support, without which we could not bring this book to life. Broken to Brilliant is thankful to have secured a $16,700 Social Investment Grant. Community Sector Banking's annual Social Investment Grants Program shows the power for good that everyday banking can have in the community. This grant will fund the printed book and ebook, as well as an audio book and podcasts to provide resources in many forms to help rebuild the lives of people who have survived domestic abuse.

During the development of *Shattered to Shining* we reached a new level in our mission of domestic violence survivors mentoring fellow survivors. The four-day live-in writing workshop was facilitated and supported primarily by domestic violence survivors and authors from our previous books. This is our 'paying it forward' model in action, supporting fellow survivors to create a new chapter in their lives.

The live-in workshop days are long and we thank the writing workshop presenters and supporters, many of whom are domestic violence survivors:

- Belinda Pollard, Small Blue Dog Publishing
- Kerry Tuck, art therapist, Broken to Brilliant, author and speaker
- Nicola Coleman, Broken to Brilliant, author and speaker
- Colin Hancock, Broken to Brilliant, author and speaker
- Linda Sawrey, Director Broken to Brilliant, Psychotherapist, Equine Assisted Therapist, author and speaker
- Andrea Miller, Co-Founding Director Broken to Brilliant, author and speaker
- Kate Smith, Founding Director Broken to Brilliant, author and speaker
- Fiona Ware, women's advocate, facilitator and children's author and speaker
- Mercy Place and their supportive, caring staff.

Also, thank you to:

- those who wrote a testimonial, reading the book in a short time frame and providing your heartfelt reflections.
- the narrators who have donated their time and voices to the chapters of *Shattered to Shining*. To ensure the anonymity and safety of each author we cannot list which chapter each voice artist has narrated.
- those who have shared how the books have helped them. These are the words of encouragement that fuel our dedication to bring this roadmap of healing to life.

FOREWORD

The authors of *Shattered to Shining* are battle worn and brave. Despite all that was thrown at them, they didn't give up. The resilience and courage of these authors never ceases to amaze me. I feel incredibly privileged to have personally met them, and watched in awe as they transformed their experiences of the past into the chapters of this book. Reading their stories, I have been both deeply moved and disturbingly unsettled by the journeys these remarkable, resilient people have been on.

These chapters will for many of us open our eyes to the sense of absolute hopelessness of the vicious cycle, and the enormity of what it takes to break the cycle. What makes it even harder to digest is that the suffering and the struggle was through the hands of those that cared for and loved them.

Many of these relationships began with fluttering excitement, joy and a world full of possibilities, as they were swept off their feet. Gradual disbelief and foggy confusion emerged as they grapple with the tiny slivers of doubt, before the ugly reality of abuse dawned on them.

These authors shone so brightly before their journey into domestic and family violence, and it was as if their shining light drew the abusers to them. They are compassionate, caring and beautiful souls. It makes what happens to them even more confusing and incomprehensible as it goes against their very core.

They teetered on the edge between awareness and denial as trust and safety gradually eroded.

The bright, beautiful, shining souls in this book open their hearts with such raw openness that reaches out to us. As I read their stories their pain and suffering was tangible. It sent shivers down my spine, my heart raced, tears welled in my eyes as their words reached out to me – as they will to you. Their struggle is immense, often alone, with very little hope. Yet despite the almost unsurmountable struggle they have soared above it and continued on their journey of finding their light again.

They are reconnecting with life, revitalising the feeling and meaning of what it is to be alive. Alive in every cell of their body, every second and every breath. This is an incredible feat as the very things they held dear were often specifically targeted by the abuser, and have been buried very deep, almost forgotten. The authors share with you what it takes – how they breathed life back into themselves, so that we can all learn and grow. How they clawed their way back to safety, connection and trust, and found their passion and purpose in life again.

We glimpse their struggle and the wisdom that arose from their journey. They help us understand the lead up into the relationship, the flags, so that for others they can be recognised and addressed early for what they are, rather than pushed aside, ignored or dismissed. Hindsight can be a torturous regret that serves very little purpose for those who have already experienced the event, but can provide powerful lessons for the rest of us to learn from. These stories should be read by all of us, even those who are responsible for this suffering.

These stories show how the authors were able to take the huge step to end the cycle of abuse. To step off the crazy merry-go-round, even when the potential price was enormous. Their courage is astounding. How they picked up all the fragmented bits of themselves, as their world disintegrated around them, and moved forward with such bravery.

Reading their joy as they rediscovered and recreated a new self with the pieces of the shattered past warmed my heart. I felt as if I was cheering with them, my heart glowing with pride as I saw their smiles, heard their laughter and watched the light finally shine from their eyes. Their sense of hope shines bright as they reconnect with themselves, their world and those around them. To have come out of such a dark place and to blossom in such remarkable ways is astounding.

These stories need to be told in rawness and authenticity, from the heart, by sharing lived experience. As readers we need to open our minds, and challenge our own outdated beliefs that allow these behaviours to exist in our society. We need to really listen, no matter how uncomfortable this make us, no matter how much we prefer to block it out or turn a blind eye, if there is to be any chance that the future can be free of domestic violence.

As individuals, families, friends, workplaces and communities, we all play a vital role in this change. We are all responsible for ensuring the words and the wisdom that stem from these stories are shared far and wide. These words had been left unsaid for far too long. There has been too much suffering and the price paid for the silence is too great.

This question I ask you: Do you have the courage to join

these authors in sharing their stories far and wide so that none of us live in an unsafe world? Help build a world where we are free to shine.

Linda
Author, Speaker, Director of Broken to Brilliant

CONTENTS

PRAISE FOR SHATTERED TO SHINING iii

THANK YOU xiii

FOREWORD xvii

INTRODUCTION 1

CHAPTER ONE
    The glue of self-love 17

CHAPTER TWO
    Your spirit is your true shield 35

CHAPTER THREE
    Warrior 47

CHAPTER FOUR
    Champagne tastes 63

CHAPTER FIVE
    The steps to your future self 79

CHAPTER SIX
    Your new life is within your grasp 98

CHAPTER SEVEN
  Believing in myself 111

CHAPTER EIGHT
  My pot of gold at the end of the rainbow 126

CHAPTER NINE
  Finding space to be me 141

CHAPTER TEN
  Home at last 159

CHAPTER ELEVEN
  Loss, grief, despair – repair with gratitude 176

CHAPTER TWELVE
  The impact of writing my story 187

GLOSSARY 202

CONTACT NUMBERS 205

ENDNOTES 211

INTRODUCTION

'Imagining the possibilities, that was what kept me alive – what was in my future. Hold onto a sense of adventure and embrace that!'

As I walked into the writing retreat, I thought, 'You have to be kidding me, this is not happening!' I came here with huge barriers. It freaked me out, being with strangers and having to trust. I realised that my biggest fear was being vulnerable and having no armour on whatsoever.

The theme of the weekend was the journey away from being shattered to shining. So I said, 'Stuff it! Get your a__ back in there.'

I knew I was among a very special group of people. We survived our abusers. There was an invisible golden thread of hope that connected us all.

This is what it is all about: being incredibly resilient, surviving the crap in our lives, being brave and courageous for stepping out of our comfort zones and embracing our vulnerability.

What I did not expect from the weekend retreat was that becoming vulnerable with everyone would start my healing and allow me to be seen. That is where my shining came into play – it's about me having the courage to be me.

I am still on a journey of discovery to make the changes I

believe I need to make. Life and experience are an ongoing project. I feel like I have changed so much that I do not recognise who this person is. That is refreshing, honest, and I am now really me.

∗∗∗

The charity Broken to Brilliant was founded by domestic violence survivors for fellow survivors. We knew only too well that there was limited support for our long-term recovery. We help people rebuild their lives, using personal experiences and stories to share the journey that lies ahead. We combine the survivor-mentor model, mutual rehabilitation and storytelling into a pay-it-forward model by holding live-in writing retreats and publishing stories of strength and success.

It is therapeutic for survivors to share their life story in a way that doesn't deny the trauma but conveys the person's strengths and resilience. They describe their survival and the solutions they put in place to recover after adversity.[1] Voicing personal experience and using creative expression as a self-help tool[2] can facilitate healing from the trauma of domestic violence.[3] Stories of survival, recovery and remaking of self following domestic and family violence have been found to be empowering.[4]

These are the very reasons for our series of books on rebuilding life after domestic violence. We are creating connections between survivors and shared roadmaps for the journey of rebuilding life. Approaching the story in this way helps to restore hope for both the survivor and the readers.

What is family and domestic violence?

Domestic and family violence is emotional, social, financial, verbal, sexual, and physical abuse, where one family member dominates and controls the other. In most cases, the offender is male and the victim female.[5][6] They control their partner through fear, violence or threatening behaviour.[7] This is a repeated pattern or cycle of behaviour that escalates over time, slowly eroding the victim's confidence and ability to leave.[8]

The National Council to Reduce Violence against Women and their Children linked the following behaviours with domestic and family violence:

- **Emotional abuse** – blaming the victim for all problems in the relationship; constantly comparing the victim with others to undermine self-esteem and self-worth; sporadic sulking; withdrawing all interest and engagement (for example, weeks of silence); emotional blackmail.
- **Verbal abuse** – swearing and continual humiliation, either in private or in public, with attacks following clear themes that focus on intelligence, sexuality, body image, and capacity as a parent and spouse.
- **Social abuse** – systematic isolation from family and friends through techniques such as ongoing rudeness to family and friends to alienate them; instigating and controlling the move to a location where the victim has no established social circle or employment opportunities; and forbidding or physically preventing the victim from going out and meeting people.
- **Economic abuse** – complete control of all money,

including forbidding access to bank accounts; providing only an inadequate 'allowance'; not allowing the victim/survivor to seek or hold employment; and using all wages earned by the victim for household expenses.

- **Psychological abuse** – driving dangerously; destruction of property; abuse of pets in front of family members; making threats regarding custody of any children; asserting that the police and justice system will not assist, support or believe the victim; and denying an individual's reality.
- **Spiritual abuse** – denial and/or misuse of religious beliefs or practices to force victims into subordinate roles; or misuse of religious or spiritual traditions to justify physical violence or other forms of abuse.
- **Physical abuse** – includes direct assault on the body (strangulation or choking, shaking, eye injuries, slapping, pushing, spitting, punching, or kicking); use of weapons, including objects; assault of children; locking the victim out of the house; and sleep and food deprivation.
- **Sexual abuse** – any form of pressured/unwanted sex or sexual degradation by an intimate partner or ex-partner, such as sexual activity without consent; causing pain during sex; assaulting genitals; coercive sex without protection against pregnancy or sexually transmitted disease; making the victim perform sexual acts unwillingly (including taking explicit photos without their consent); criticising, or using sexually degrading insults.[9]

The red flags

Often, we struggle to recognise the signs of domestic violence, which is why the signs of abuse have been given the name 'red flags'. We need to take notice of the red flag behaviours and not be dismissive – these are warning you of a controlling, abusive person.[10][11][12][13]

These behaviours can be grouped into key themes[14]:

Charming
- they seem very thoughtful, considerate, caring, and understanding; you, your family and friends think they are wonderful.

Emotional abuse
- continuous criticism and humiliation in front of other people
- emotional blackmail – for example, 'If you loved me, you would …'
- ignoring or refusing to talk
- losing their temper frequently over little things
- speeding the relationship up – quickly moving in together or opening joint bank accounts
- making you feel as if you are walking on eggshells to keep the peace
- playing mind games or making you feel guilty
- refusing to take responsibility for their actions – blaming you, drugs or alcohol for their behaviour.

Controlling
- monitoring what you are doing – going through your text messages, emails and social media
- using technology to track where you are
- telling you to check in with them regularly
- telling you what to wear, where you can go, and who you can spend time with
- controlling how much money you have or preventing you from getting a job
- threatening you with weapons and/or to hurt or kill you, the children, family or the pets
- threatening to publish private information
- refusing to use birth control or protection
- jealousy – accusing you of having affairs.

Isolation
- discouraging or preventing you from seeing family, friends, or work colleagues outside of work; isolating you from other people
- preventing you from practising religion
- encouraging you to spend more and more time with them
- moving you long distances away.

Physical abuse
- shoving, pushing, tripping, pinching, spitting, hair pulling
- close-up, in-your-face screaming
- holding you down and ejaculating over you

- causing injuries such as scratches, bruises, and broken bones
- kicking or punching; hurting pets
- strangulation.

If you recognise these signs and behaviours, you need to get help from trained professionals who can work with you to keep you safe while you exit the relationship. See useful contact numbers on page 205.

Family and domestic violence statistics

Every country is battling the scourge of domestic and family violence. The World Health Organisation reviewed data from over 80 countries and found that one in three women (about 35%) have experienced physical and/or sexual violence by an intimate partner, or non-partner sexual violence.

Worldwide, the amount of family and domestic violence experienced is alarming:

- In the United States, an average of 20 people experience intimate partner physical violence every minute. This equates to more than 10 million abuse victims annually.[15]
- In England and Wales, it is estimated that 7.9% of women (1.3 million) and 4.2% of men (695,000) experienced domestic abuse.[16]
- In Europe, one in three women have experienced some form of physical and/or sexual violence since the age of 15. Just over one in five women have experienced physical and/or sexual violence from either a current or previous partner, whilst 43% of women have experienced

some form of psychologically abusive and/or controlling behaviour when in a relationship.[17]
- In Africa, more than one in three women (36.6%) report having experienced physical and/or sexual partner violence, or sexual violence by a non-partner. Six African countries have no legal protection for women against domestic violence: Burkina Faso, Cote d'Ivoire, Egypt, Lesotho, Mali and Niger.[18]
- In Russia, more than 600 women are killed each month in their own homes, and up to 36,000 women a day are being abused.[19] In 2017, Russia decriminalised some forms of domestic violence.[20]
- In Asia, 21–55% of women report experiencing physical and/or sexual violence by an intimate partner in their lifetime.[21]
- In Australia, 2.2 million adults have been victims of physical and/or sexual violence from a partner since the age of 15. One in two women and one in four men have been sexually harassed, and one in six women and one in 16 men have experienced stalking. In 2017, police recorded 25,000 victims of sexual assault. There were 26,500 children aged 0–9 who were assisted by specialist homelessness services due to domestic violence in 2017–18. Every nine days, one woman is killed and every 29 days one man is killed as a result of domestic violence.[22]

The impact of family and domestic violence

When you leave, everyone thinks it stops. It does not stop. Some leave safely, and the abuse stops. For others, the abuse escalates and continues after they have left. When you are finally free, and you have stopped holding yourself together for survival, you can start to unravel; you begin to realise the impact that domestic and family violence has had on you and your children.

It affects your everyday life, wellbeing and aspirations. You will need help from family, friends and services for accommodation. Many will have to find new jobs, new homes, a new suburb, city or state to live in to be safe from their abuser. The life you once knew, your home, your friends, your children's school, your sporting, social and spiritual life – GONE. You may have lost connection with yourself and your community.

For these reasons, survivors can be overcome by an enormous sense of grief and loss. Their experiences can lead to depression, anxiety and a range of other mental and physical health issues.[23] One study found that the physical and mental health of women who experienced domestic violence was 'consistently worse' after 16 years than those who had not experienced abuse, and these effects can last a lifetime.[24]

We need men and women of all ages to work together through RESPECTFUL relationships to break the violence. Radical change and transformation of our society is needed now, so that future generations

Respectful

Relationships
Emotionally
Supportive
Positive
Enriching
Caring
Togetherness
Friendship
Understanding
Love

won't have the level of terror and tragedy that we are dealing with daily.

The impact of our series of books

There is a gap in the research on the post-abuse journey. How do survivors of domestic violence fully achieve psychological and physical wellbeing as they encounter the demands of creating a new life?[25][26][27][28]

The Royal Commission into Family Violence (2016) found that the 'current responses to family violence do not sufficiently emphasise recovery and restoration and may even impede it. The ultimate objective of the family violence system must be that victims, including children, can recover and thrive at their own pace'.[29]

Helping fellow domestic violence survivors in their journey after domestic violence is something we undertake from the knowledge of our lived experience: survivors mentoring fellow survivors. There is very little known about the coping strategies used by survivors post abuse. As survivors we know this, and we have been sharing our journeys. Through the combination of tear-stained pages and keyboards, we have shared the steps to rebuilding life after domestic violence in three books. Across this series are stories from 32 survivors, sharing over 96,000 words about their abuse and how to rebuild their lives.

For each book, we received more applicants' stories than we could fit into one book. For some of those survivors, they were still in unsafe situations and their journey was still too raw. Is there a right time? An exact number of months or years to be able to share your story? No, time is not the key factor.

Is there recovery after abuse? 'Recovery is not defined by the complete absence of thoughts or feelings about the traumatic experience but being able to live with it in a way that it isn't in control of your life.'[30] 'Recovery from family violence is an ongoing journey, a process of survival, of finding "self" and becoming free from the fear and suffering caused by the trauma of family violence.'[31] The journey of surviving and thriving occurs over time; it is chaotic, emotional, and unique to each person. As survivors, our stories bear resemblance and our steps of healing may be similar, although each person walks their spiralled path their own way.

Broken to Brilliant

In 2016, we proudly launched our first book in this series, *Broken to Brilliant: Breaking Free to Be You After Domestic Violence, Stories of Strength and Success.* Through generous donations to our 'Give a Book' campaign and through grants, hundreds of these books have been gifted to domestic violence survivors in shelters and refuges, or to other services that support domestic violence survivors as they rebuild their lives.

Are these stories beneficial? **Our survey found that readers said** the book was inspiring and helpful. It educated them about domestic violence and strategies to rebuild lives. Most readers reported that they experienced personal growth after reading this self-help book.

We received encouraging words, such as: the book *'gives hope to others experiencing domestic violence and the choices they can make to have a new beginning.'*

The ten *Broken to Brilliant* writers said they would recommend the writing process to other survivors, as they found that writing their story helped to turn a bad experience into a good one. It gave meaning to their experience, set them free and helped them to focus on the positives of what they have achieved. Knowing their story was going to serve others in the same situation made the process humbling and added a sense of purpose and worth to their lives. They felt honoured to be involved.

'It showed me that there was value to my life and my story and that I can turn my pain into purpose to help serve others.'

Professionals who work in refuges and shelters have said that they have found the book very helpful, as women can relate to the stories and the stories are all different. They use the book as a sample to help other women with their story and to comfort them, supporting women towards resilience. Their clients have said:

- 'This sounds like my story.'
- 'Can I take the book with me when I leave?'
- 'This book gives me hope that I can get through this.'

The book received a bronze award in the self-help category of the eLit awards, a global program committed to illuminating and honouring the very best of English-language digital publishing.

Terror to Triumph

The book *Broken to Brilliant* had a positive impact on people's lives – it breathed hope into people's hearts and inspired the spark of a new chapter in their lives. These stories created ripples of recovery and repair – we could not turn away and stop these ripples of healing.

And so, the concept for *Terror to Triumph* emerged.

We wanted to enhance our support for the authors, so this time we held a three-day live-in writing retreat. Eleven women and one man attended. Activities included art therapy, writing techniques, exercise, meditation and positive affirmation. The activities helped participants recover their ability to play, plan, laugh, create, hope and write.

The authors said that the support we provided felt authentic, they felt loved, valued and heard, which built trust among the group. The retreat changed them and their thinking. They left feeling more confident, encouraged and open to alternative self-care methods. One person said, *'I leave a different person. There is no doubt about that.'*

From the workshop, they were able to reconnect with their stories in a way that enabled them to focus more on what they had overcome and achieved in rebuilding their lives, rather than what they had experienced during the abuse. This enabled a clearer expression and understanding of the strategies survivors implemented as part of their rebuilding process.

Twelve brave authors stepped forward to share their stories of the terror experienced and the practical steps taken on their recovery and how they reclaimed self to reach a sense of triumph.

'I had an overwhelming sense of belonging, which was both uncomfortable but welcomed.'

Shattered to Shining

Once again, we were inspired to embark on another book, due to the amazing breakthroughs the authors reported as a result of the *Terror to Triumph* writing retreat and sharing their stories.

The third book was made possible thanks to a grant from the Community Banking Sector. With the funds for the publishing costs of the print, ebook, an audiobook and podcast, the charity was able to call for author applications for *Shattered to Shining*. Reading their stories, you will gain a connection to each of the authors, as they share their story and their pain of being shattered from abuse, and their relief and aliveness as they shine again.

It was a profound pleasure to meet the brave, resilient authors at the *Shattered to Shining* four-day live-in writing workshop. After this packed weekend, all authors agreed that the activities were helpful, useful, worthwhile, supportive, and well organised and facilitated. **What they said they found most valuable** about the workshop included the:

- different therapies offered – writing, art, music, exercise, writing coaching, meditation, group sharing

- connections they made, with no judgement and so much support
- other survivors they met and sharing experiences
- support provided by the facilitators
- time away from everything to focus on themselves.

The experience of bringing their stories to life has been a roller-coaster ride of oscillating emotions, from the depths of despair for the pain they endured to the elation at how they are now shining bright. In the authors' words:

- 'It was through writing the chapter that I located my younger inner-child and was able to commence the healing process for her. Lots of healing tears flowed … as I was able to voice her pain and fears …'
- 'The Broken to Brilliant team helped my recovery. I had planned to review my chapter yesterday but couldn't. I did so today and couldn't believe the amazing editing. I felt really proud and supported, so thank you all from the bottom of my heart. Once again I was in tears – happy tears.'
- 'What I did not expect from this weekend and I've realised is … I have started healing myself.'
- 'I'm very grateful as always to the Broken to Brilliant team. Each and every one of you make a huge difference to so many.'
- 'I'm so grateful to have the opportunity to pour my story into words to help others! I hope it does! As I edited it and did the final read, I imagined someone reading

it – just one person – and as they close the pages they think, "OK, I'm going to get started!"'

Get started on your journey away from abuse – there is a world of happiness shining brightly for you to join.

CHAPTER ONE

THE GLUE OF SELF-LOVE

'Recovery takes reconnecting, healing and rebuilding a broken self, in a world that's also shattered. Putting everything back together means finding those many pieces and finding the glue of self-love that can hold everything together.'

FALLING TO MY KNEES, I REACHED UP TO HIM. 'PLEASE!' I CRIED in desperation. 'Please, give me my car keys.' I had been trying to quit smoking but couldn't do it – not today. I needed to get cigarettes. My life was a cesspool, my mind swimming in disturbing thoughts. I didn't want to be alive.

His tall, menacing 130 kilograms loomed over my 58 kg body. In one hand, he held my keys. The other jabbed a pointed finger in my face. 'You're just a pathetic, weak, piece of s___!' he laughed.

Our children stood upstairs, watching and crying. They screamed, 'Stop doing that to my mum! Help!'

We were isolated in our bushland home, so no-one heard.

Waking the next morning, I knew the day wouldn't be a kind one. What I didn't know was that it would mark the beginning of the end. This would be the first day in over ten years I found the courage to leave.

***

For a long time, he had been openly flirting in front of me and then justifying his behaviour: 'You have jealousy problems.' He progressed from suggestive innuendos to putting on pornography with other couples there. Eventually, he was coercing everyone to get touchy, or to have sex in front of each other. He began these nights pressuring me into getting drunk. Sometimes I'd sneak to bed. Sometimes I gave in. Life was easier that way and I thought he'd grow out of it.

One night, a friend of many years visited with her husband for drinks – although I wasn't drinking. She was the only person I'd allowed a glimpse behind my closed doors. I'd disclosed the uncertain future of my marriage.

Late that evening, my drunk husband proposed swapping wives. My friend didn't seem to mind, but I felt objectified as he pressured her husband to go f__ me. I refused and went to bed completely disconcerted. Waking up alone, I discovered my husband and 'friend' had slept together anyway.

'Swinging' was a whole new level of perversion. When I refused the swinging, he manipulated me with the fear of how he would treat my children and me when he didn't get his way. Too exhausted, I lost my voice. My life, a constant compromise of my integrity, revolved around keeping him happy. I just wanted peace. I felt trapped, with nothing left, no fight, no hope.

Demoralised and defeated, I became less reactive, retreating into a crushing world of extreme sadness. This undermined his ability to create the drama that he thrived on, and he became more excruciatingly controlling – and cruel.

***

The morning after he tormented me with the car keys, he yanked the blanket off me. 'Get out of bed, f___ing lazy b___!' He relentlessly unleashed tormenting taunts and savage threats. I refused to react and engage. I don't remember any of his words; I just remember how the fear they evoked nauseated me.

Things had become progressively worse. The cycle of abuse would turn full circle anywhere from a couple of times per month up to a number of times a day. The threats and physical abuse had increased to a point where I feared for our safety.

I made a plan. I packed a bag of kids' things, hiding it near the back door. I intended to sneak it to the car, but he began following me everywhere around the house, so the opportunity never arose.

I waited agonisingly all day for a time I thought would be safe. I told him I was taking the kids to get takeaway for dinner. He stood, glaring threateningly at me as I drove away. I felt guilty, as though I'd done something wrong.

With four young children, feeling desperately alone, everything seemed surreal. I was ashamed to tell anyone, afraid that no-one would believe me.

In an overwhelmed fog, I'd planned to go but had not planned where. I found myself at my 'friend's' home. If she'd believed me in the past, she obviously didn't believe me now. She wouldn't listen.

She told him I was there.

I returned home to him after one night ... absolutely shattered.

***

Growing up in a small town, I left home at 17 – unhappy and obviously ill-equipped to recognise red flags. I was in my twenties and he was unhappily engaged when he first began pursuing me. Our first date was on the same day he separated from his fiancée.

He'd already purchased a car, boat, motorcycle, and a home. It was thrilling receiving expensive gifts, but it was more the feeling that he 'completed' me that attracted me. He took control, was confident, assertive and spontaneous – all the things I wasn't.

It only took a couple of his sad childhood stories for me to latch on with my empathetic need to 'save' people. Out poured my life story, exposing every insecurity and vulnerability. I craved validation, and felt I wasn't a full person by myself. I hated being alone with my own sad, damaged company.

I moved in within three months. Immediately, he began to take away my independence. Within two years I'd quit my job and sold my car, to help him start his business. I became completely dependent on him. Moving to acreage conveniently isolated me, but he was all I needed anyway.

Starting a family was the result of a fight. An apologetic, romantic picnic restored my faith. 'I'm sorry, I didn't mean it. I never want to be with anyone else. Let's make a baby.' He loved me.

I laughed it off when my pregnant body repulsed him, and he refused to touch my belly. 'That's okay, that's just him. Ha-ha.'

I was 38 weeks pregnant when we spent a few nights away. Bored with me, he went out for the afternoon, coming back intoxicated and savage. Like knives, his words cut me deeply, and the way he stood his intimidating frame over my vulnerable body was terrifying. He was 'just drunk'. It wouldn't happen again.

I believed he'd change, if I just made him understand how I felt. Instead, insecurities and feelings became ammunition to gaslight me and shift blame. 'Sour b____. You're too sensitive. You're the problem.' He'd project what he was guilty of: 'Stop controlling me! You're cheating on me!' I was constantly explaining and defending myself.

Every apology, promise, new possession, property or holiday reignited hope that he'd change.

I'd try to parent with some structure and routine. He'd undermine me, belittle me and involve the kids. Ganging up on me, they'd reduce me to tears. He liked making me cry. Now THEY were just trying to keep him happy. I was losing my authority as Mum.

He'd stop me comforting my children when they were distressed. Their eyes emanated pain that pierced my heart. I'd wait until he was asleep and go into their bedrooms. I'd stroke their faces while they slept, and cry for them. Sometimes my mind became numb, disconnected, unable to cope with the debilitating pain, shame and guilt of what my children were experiencing.

When he got physical he was always 'just angry' ... like anger actually justifies breaking wooden spoons across children's bare bottoms; or smacking someone across the head; or stripping your child, calling them a stupid little c___ and locking them outside; or backhanding them in the stomach.

Or it was always 'just a joke' … because apparently it's hilarious to smother someone with a pillow; choke them with a tea towel; slam the brakes on, smashing heads into dashboards; slap, punch, kick, throw things at people …

But his words left the worst wounds. Deeply-embedded scars on our minds no-one could see. Even we couldn't see.

As he increasingly told me I was 'useless', 'pathetic', 'nothing without him', 'psycho b___', 'slut' … I started thinking this WASN'T okay. When he told me he could easily snap my arm or leg, throw me over the railing, or drown me in the dam and make it look like an accident … this WASN'T funny and WASN'T a joke. When he withheld money, then abused me for using a credit card for food and bills … this WASN'T fair. When he told me to f___ off out of HIS house but also said, if I left him, he'd kill me or make my life hell, take my children away and put me in a mental institution … this WAS POSSIBLY ABUSE?

***

My first huge wake-up call came from a man I've never met, from halfway around the world. Amazing that he could have such a profound influence on me. I saw my life being played out on a TV show. I heard Dr Phil tell a crying woman that her husband was an abusive narcissist, and she needed to leave him. I was gutted.

Confronting questions harassed every thought. How had I

become swallowed up by this insidious, toxic world? Was I that obtuse? Was this real? Was this my fault? Was I crazy? I felt stupid and ashamed, my world disintegrating.

Caught in the same strange web of deceit and manipulation, a connection had formed between my 'friend's' husband and me. Respectful and kind, he replaced his wife as my best friend and only confidant. We'd talk, and he'd actually listen, telling me my husband's disrespect was not okay, inadvertently showing me a glimpse of how I deserved to be treated, becoming another catalyst to my departure.

Two days before I left, my child found me hiding, and crying, after another verbal beating. My child said, 'Mum, just say sorry.' I said, 'I haven't done anything wrong.' They replied, 'Just say sorry, he'll be happy, and it'll be over'… my child was ten years old.

What the hell was I teaching my children? They were growing up to follow in my footsteps. I was done.

I told my best friend I was leaving, also saying goodbye to him. The friendship was obviously too complicated to continue. Then I told his wife. I thought she needed to know, because this meant she and her husband would be returning to their 'normal' life …

'We've wanted to be together for a long time,' was her response. My husband had seen this coming and had already asked her to move in … into MY home. The shock and betrayal sent me into a stupefied blur of crisis. Then, self-preservation saw an opportunity.

Maybe if he had her, he'd be less focused on me. Maybe this

would save me from the things he'd threatened to do. In a tortured daze, I helped her move into my home and, believing I had no other choice, I became homeless.

I never sought support services and had no family close. Confused and ashamed, I didn't know what to tell people anyway. I was afraid of speaking up about the abuse. He'd told me it wasn't true and no-one would believe me.

One piece of advice someone told me provided invaluable ammunition in the fight for my children. It was to make sure you **document absolutely everything**.

***

After leaving the abuse, control and manipulation continued. The stress of standing up to him made me physically ill. The dense fog in my mind made rational thought difficult. Thinking he'd act fairly and we'd be able to co-parent was completely ridiculous.

He'd withhold money, reducing me to the humiliation of begging. I was ineligible for financial assistance or legal aid, because of assets in my name. A few mums from my kids' school provided some food and clothes. One lady provided me shelter.

I insisted on having my kids stay with me every second week, but they struggled with the arrangements. While I could barely feed them, they were receiving gifts, dining out and holidaying with their father and stepmother.

Time, and a lifting fog, revealed the truth about their relationship. A year previously, when he'd sensed I was waking up, he'd lined up my replacement. The 'swinging' had been a collaboration between them, enabling a validated affair, eliminating the need to hide.

After two months I had to move, with no choice other than the home of my abuser's parents. His father constantly criticised me, trying to manipulate my decisions. He even tried convincing me that leaving town, without my kids, would be good for me and everyone else.

We needed to get out of there – we needed a home.

I found a suitable property but was unsure when I'd have funds. Not wanting to waste the owner's time, I told them I was unable to purchase. They asked if something was wrong. Breaking down, I spilled my dilemma.

For the first time, I was honest and vulnerable **safely, with kind people**, having no hopes or expectations. Previously, I had been vulnerable **unsafely with a narcissist**, expecting kindness and hoping to be loved.

What happened then was astounding. They dropped the price $70,000. They said they'd wait until I had the money. They even prayed for me. My faith in human kindness was a little restored.

***

With his father's help, my husband used my desperation to his advantage. Threatening to further withhold funds, he coerced me into signing court orders, allowing him 50% custody. It was a devastating mistake. I got our home, but then began my most heartbreaking battle.

My children, now his main focus of control, endured his slander campaign, his attempts to alienate me. He manipulated the two older children to live primarily with him. Each child played a role in the cruel, narcissistic competition to win Dad's 'love'.

My nine-year-old described how he'd laugh, while using one child to beat up another. 'We're just a game to him, Mum, something for him to play with.'

Over the next five years I shattered many times as I tried to get legal, child safety or police help. No-one could – or would – help me. Learning about support services, I utilised every one to the extent I could. The serious lack of understanding of domestic violence and its associated trauma is alarming. Systems and services meant to assist and protect are flawed and full of gaps.

Every time I fell and thought I couldn't get back up, I rose – just a little smarter and a little stronger than before.

***

The fog in my mind for so long gnarled my sense of reality, like a distorted mirror. I still questioned my perception, judgement and sanity. I was desperate to make sense of my world, grasp an understanding of who I was, and who or what he was.

I researched abuse, narcissism, complex trauma, co-dependence, and started studying a diploma. Feeling more empowered with knowledge and understanding, I began educating my kids on how to recognise subtle forms of mistreatment. I refused any more physical or verbal contact from him.

I took away his opportunity to disempower me, and initiated mediation.

With my eyes leaking the entire six hours, the joint session was incredibly traumatic and achieved nothing. When he left, I wailed, feeling devastatingly weak. The mediators said, 'You held it together so long. You didn't break until he'd left. You've shown amazing strength and should be incredibly proud of what you've done.' This validation, something that had been lacking my entire life, meant an incredible amount.

My many reports to Child Safety achieved nothing. Unsure how to protect my children, I applied for a family violence protection order. Because we were one year post 'no contact', the abuse was considered 'historical'. Hurting me through the children made it 'indirect'. Obtaining the order was difficult, but I succeeded. I had **very specific details** from **everything I'd documented**. This made him scared. This gave me power, made me stronger.

After two and a half years, my eldest child came back to me. 'It just clicked one day,' they said. 'The abuse stuff you taught us – I realised that was my life.' My child had wanted to leave for months but was too scared.

They told me, 'When the mediation person interviewed us kids, Dad made me record it on my phone.' He'd punished them for telling me about the concerns I'd brought up in the joint session. My 13-year-old child said, 'He made me read all that stuff you wrote for court [my affidavit] and help him write his.' I was mortified.

I joined a women's support group. While my domestic violence knowledge was now extensive, I hadn't grasped the imperativeness of self-care. As I began exploring this concept, everything changed again. I now had all my children full-time, two refusing any paternal contact.

As they struggled with trauma and confusion, another kind,

sensitive child began mirroring their father, and disconnecting from me. The mediation psychologist had been concerned this was happening, urging their father to encourage the relationship with me … but disconnection was his intent.

Days before I lost this child, while we were driving to mother-child counselling, I said, 'Saying you've been mistreated doesn't mean you don't love Dad.' They said, 'I can't remember.' I replied, 'What do you mean? You've told me—'

'You don't understand,' my child interrupted. 'I CAN'T remember. It hurts too much.' This child was also only 13.

My husband's cruel words poured from my child's mouth. Things were thrown and smashed, threats were made, knives pulled. Home became a toxic mix of anger, sadness, trauma triggers and conflict. I used up all my oxygen trying to breathe for everyone, hold everyone together.

Desperate for help, I found only a failing system. 'We've no suggestions to add to supports you already have in place, there's nothing we can do.' Child Safety sent my child back to the abuser.

Destroyed, I escaped nightly with wine. Three traumatised children mourned the loss of their sibling. I fell victim to my grief, and became a slave to my addiction. I'd failed. I wanted to die. My mind's narrative asked, 'How much more can I take?'

It would be weeks before the love I have for my kids finally empowered me to leave the house again. He'd said I was useless and pathetic – I didn't want to prove him right. Attending a self-compassion workshop was the first time I'd felt remotely alive since the women's group seven months earlier.

I made a colossal commitment. Signing up for a five-week course became the catalyst for a life-changing shift. We delved into an array of self-focused tasks. Rediscovering me and facing the mirror of self-reflection was confronting. The awareness that came from 'facing me' began to guide me down the road of recovery and healing, and was wonderfully liberating.

Everything I began to explore, combined with all I'd learnt and experienced, formed a collaboration of hope. My mindset flipped from devastated to inspired, and from defeated to determined.

I stopped drinking, just like that. I was no longer failing. Instead of asking, 'How much more can I take?', I was thinking of how much I could give. I wanted to work with youth, share what I wish my younger self had known, be who I'd needed. I found purpose.

***

Throughout my youth, I hadn't understood the concept of consent, healthy boundaries, or the rights I had over my own body. I was 13 when my first boyfriend took my virginity. It wasn't consensual ... neither were many other encounters with boys. Some I'd just let happen, even if I didn't want to. Some were forced. I just wanted to feel loved but didn't understand this wasn't love. I didn't know how to say 'no' or 'stop', or recognise controlling or covertly abusive behaviours. I'd blame myself, hate myself, and think it was normal to feel alone and sad most of the time.

Contemplating where I'd come from helped me understand this wasn't my fault.

From these beginnings, my choices eventuated in more than

ten years of toxic co-dependence. Being defensive and numbing myself made me emotionally unavailable. This prevented the strong, healthy connections necessary for relationships and overall wellness. Coping by repressing hard feelings, denying the wounds exist, or filling the cracks with alcohol, was like feeding a festering infection. It can't heal and will continue to cause pain.

Exploring where I'd been showed me there's no place for blame, guilt and shame. These prevented me taking the responsibility to move forward and do better. My children and I were damaged. I couldn't change the past but I could choose to change our future.

I surrendered to authenticity and honesty, learning to be open to feeling and accepting all emotions. Leaving my wounds open with vulnerability also opened my mind, along with my heart. I learnt that freedom and healing were waiting for me.

I let myself feel the pain but refused to let it swallow me, and I forgave myself. I found compassion for the damaged little girl I'd been, and for the perfectly imperfect woman I've become. My open wounds let out the hurt but also allowed in the beauty of hope, love, peace, and joy.

Reflecting on what I know now, I understand that I am not unlovable. He is narcissistic, and incapable of love in its true sense. I feel a confidence I've never felt in my life. I don't worry if people are going to like me anymore; I wonder if I'm going to like them.

I found independence in its absolute meaning. I was incomplete because I looked externally to fill a gap, to feel love. I filled it with men, then babies ... but that love I needed had to first come FROM me, FOR me.

I found gratitude for my experiences, as they've shaped who I've become. I have the power and wisdom to break the cycle of dysfunction, and the opportunity to make a difference in the world.

For the first time in my life, I know and accept who I was and who I am. I'm safe to be and to love that person. I don't NEED anyone anymore, and I feel happiness and serenity in my own company. Now, I am complete.

***

After leaving, I expected I'd simply build a new life. When my expectations weren't met, I was unjustly hard on myself. I wish someone had been there to tell me that the levels of complexity to this journey can mean years of travel but, when you look back, you won't believe your bravery and what you were able to overcome.

Recovery takes reconnecting, healing and rebuilding a broken self in a world that's also shattered.

Putting everything back together means finding that many pieces will cut you, and some are just lost. It means finding the glue of self-love that can hold everything together.

When my course finished, the supportive environment I'd become accustomed to fell away and I experienced a sense of loss. Decluttering my house, I found a Hot Wheels car left behind by my child. I just broke.

It was like all the feelings I'd ever denied myself about my children resurfaced. Engulfed in a flood of memories and emotions,

I felt like my head would explode and my heart implode ... like I was slipping back into the deep, dark place again. But ...

When I stopped crying and got off the floor, I felt like I'd been released ... like I'd been cleansed of everything I'd repressed ... like when the rain washes the dust off the leaves on the trees, and the sun makes them glisten and shine. I realised that after spending my life switching between victim and survivor, this is what it feels like to be a thriver.

A piece of my heart is yet to return, and I know I still have storms to face ... but eventually the storm will clear my path and cleanse the pain. I'll have learnt something new, and grown a little more. I have hope, purpose, peace, love and joy, and I'm grateful.

I think the day I broke, and felt the cleansing release, marked the beginning of the next path on my journey.

My journey won't stop here because I believe I have something special to share with the world. Me.

Now that I've found my inner light, it's my time to truly shine.

FACING ME are the signposts to recovery and liberty

I couldn't change the past, but I could change our future. I wish someone had been there to tell me about the levels of complexity to this journey. That it can mean years of travel. Recovery takes reconnecting, healing and rebuilding a broken self in a world that's also shattered. Putting everything back together means finding many pieces and using the glue of self-love to hold everything together.

I travelled this road and, with support, you can too. Looking back, you won't believe your bravery, and what you were able to overcome. I've found my inner light; it's my time to truly shine. You too can shine. **FACING ME** are the signposts, to find the glue of self-love on the road to recovery and freedom.

Forgiveness: Forgive yourself and understand this wasn't your fault. Find compassion for the perfectly imperfect person you are. Open wounds let out the hurt, but also allow in the beauty of hope, love, peace, and joy.

Authenticity: Surrender to authenticity and honesty. Learn to be open to feelings and accept all emotions. Let yourself feel the pain but refuse to let it swallow you. This will mean freedom and healing will be available to you.

Counselling: Access and use counselling support services. Utilise all the services you can for yourself and your children. Join a support group.

Independence: Find independence in its absolute meaning.

Look internally to fill the gap, to feel love. The love you need is FROM you, FOR you.

Nurture: Nurture your relationship with yourself, and understand you are lovable. Develop your confidence. Don't worry if people are going to like you; wonder if you're going to like them. Know and accept who you are, that it's safe to be you and love that person. Learn to feel happiness and serenity in your own company.

Gratitude: Find gratitude in your experiences as they've shaped who you have become. Realise you have the power to break the cycle of dysfunction and the opportunity to make a difference in the world.

Move forward: Every time you fall and think you cannot get back up, love yourself enough to get back up. You are worth it and you will rise a little smarter and a little stronger than before. Keep moving forward with hope, purpose, peace, love and joy, as your journey won't stop here.

Empowerment: Knowledge is power. Educate yourself and your children on how to recognise subtle forms of mistreatment. Sign up for a course – it could be the catalyst for a life-changing shift. Find your passion to find your purpose and consider study. You will feel more empowered with knowledge and understanding. Learning about abuse, narcissism, complex trauma, and co-dependence can give you the clarity to comprehend what you have been through. Understanding can help you to heal.

© Broken to Brilliant

CHAPTER TWO

YOUR SPIRIT IS YOUR TRUE SHIELD

'Greet each day with love and joy in your heart. Your spirit is your true shield.'

DRIVING HOME FROM WORK, I FELT THAT SAME OLD SENSE OF dread. I parked the car under the house, turned off the engine and sat. The hot engine ticked like a clock marking time, and I strained my ears to hear telltale signs that would prepare me for what I was about to walk into. Would he be drunk or sober? Would there be a smile for a greeting, or would he be passed out with vomit down his shirt?

Even my breathing was too loud, so I held my breath as my ears strained to hear. Nothing. Silence. Hard to tell if this was good or bad, but there was no sound of children's little feet pitter-pattering across the floor above me.

I looked over at his car parked next to mine. Why didn't he just drive into a tree and kill himself? That would be so easy for us. I could be the grieving widow. No-one would ever have to know the truth. The truth we had been hiding for all this time.

****

I lived in a world of domestic violence when domestic violence wasn't on the radar like it is today. It was nothing for a bit of push and shove to happen. I came from a small country town which lived and breathed gossip, where judgement was high as everyone tried to outdo each other in the gossip world. I would never have opened myself and my truth to these people.

When one said the words 'domestic violence', the image that came to mind immediately was husband bashing wife. And why wouldn't it? The word 'violence' is always attuned to physical harm. When I came out about my marriage I was asked, over and over: 'Did he hit you?' Was I really in a valid domestic violence situation if I wasn't black and blue?

Doubts crept in and hung out in the corners of my mind like a bad smell and, not for the first time in my life, I questioned my own reality. What about the hours and hours that the children and I spent making sure there was nothing he could use to kickstart the cycle? Did the soul-breaking effect of psychological abuse mean anything?

***

The word 'domestic' means 'relating to family relations'. I have never really made that link until now. I have compartmentalised my life, placing certain times into individual picture frames – my childhood, my marriage, my life afterwards. If truth be known, they are all interlinked and should really be viewed as a montage or one long canvas.

I am dyslexic and as a child I struggled with my reading. When a family friend, who was staying with us for a while, offered to help me to read my school reader, I was so excited. Teeth brushed and pyjamas on I raced to my room, puffed up my pillows, and jumped into my orange cast-iron bed. My reading folder was open on my lap and I shuffled over against the wall to make room for him as we began to read. Then he placed his arm around me and put his hand down my pants. I remember freezing up and him saying to me, 'Don't you like it?'

I was seven years old. What was I supposed to say? When I told my mother, she said I was 'being ridiculous'. I asked him to stop because I didn't like it and he said he would go and read with my brother. I didn't want my brother to be subjected to the same thing, so the abuse continued.

School for me was a living hell. I was a gangly, uncoordinated child and a natural target for school bullies. By the end of my final year I had been bullied relentlessly for 12 years. There were times I was befriended, but it always ended as a cruel, hurtful joke.

I had little to no self-esteem and a really poor image of myself. I had been told I was ugly and stupid so many times that I actually believed it. When I talked to my parents about it, my mother would say how I exaggerated everything and that I was being absurd. She was quick to embarrass me by telling other people that I had 'an overactive imagination'. From that early age I felt unvalidated. I had nowhere to turn.

After coming out of my marriage, my focus was on the 'events' that happened during my time in *that* relationship. I blamed my suffering and shattered soul on *that* specific time. I have not wanted to look any further because I wanted HIM to carry the blame for the broken me. I didn't want to diminish his responsibility or give him yet another way to add credit to his claim that he was the victim. I wanted him to have the status of abuser and carry it to his grave. I have turned it over and over in my head, replaying specific events to validate my need for him to be solely responsible. I have nurtured that hate and need in my heart for many years.

The processes my brain and I have gone through over the past months, since I put my hand up for this journey with Broken to Brilliant, have brought me to an interesting place. My childhood abuse and the consequences of being open about it still scare me, even as I write this. The power of confidence starts, I believe, with knowing that you have a safe place in which to be honest, that when you fall down you do so knowing someone has your back. As a child that should be your parents, and as hard as it is for me to stand in my truth, I don't feel that I had that net of safety. I still harbour angst in my heart over the times I was disbelieved or blown off as 'being ridiculous'. My supposed overactive imagination was not seen for what it really was – perception – and consequently I was subjected to years of abuse from outside my family unit. Time after time others were believed over me until I simply pushed it all down as far as it would go. After all, I *was* ugly and stupid.

When I met my ex-husband, I was already primed for abuse.

***

I was supposed to find my prince, marry him, have beautiful babies, have the perfect house. He played the guitar and sang me love songs. We laughed and dreamed together. We were supposed to be together forever, get old and sit on the verandah to watch our grandchildren play. We should have shared little knowing smiles and had a million billion memories pass between us.

I can see now that he had a part missing that he tried to get from me and our children. Like a square peg in a round hole it just didn't fit, but for years he kept sucking the life from us, trying to fill that void in him.

I never asked myself how we got there. The dominance was so gradual, as was the loss of self, that I don't remember it happening. Thinking back, it went from a social expectation of being a 'good wife' to self-preservation and a hope to break an unbreakable cycle, or at least to stop it at a phase in which we were a normal, happy family.

Our cycle looked a little like this:

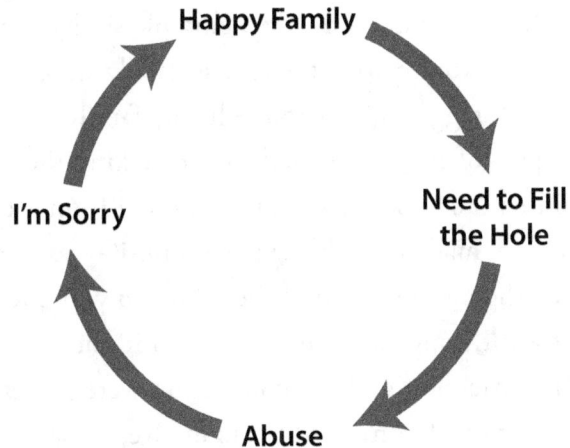

The easiest phase to understand would be the happy family, as this is what is considered normal. It was a chance to catch our breath and for the most recent wounds to be licked. There was always a sense of being on tenterhooks as we knew that the cycle would shift, despite our hopes.

The shift would start when he would begin looking for things to pick on. Any imperfections were used to point out our uselessness, and it was our uselessness that was the reason (in his eyes) that he had no choice but to turn to alcohol. No matter how hard we tried to erase any imperfections or avoid the inevitable abuse, it would come. Like a dense, wet mist it would encompass us, blind us, and make us heavy with our own faults. In the bad times, I wouldn't sleep until he was well and truly passed out – especially after I overheard a conversation with his mate when they discussed smothering me in my sleep.

The trigger for his 'I'm sorry' was always different. A cowering child, or a cold empty bed, or the car in a ditch, or a miraculous moment from me when I would scream that enough was enough. It felt to me like we were being physically strangled to the brink of blackout before it would suddenly stop.

Then we all staggered back to the happy family.

A large part of me is ashamed for not taking the right care of my children. I should have protected them from the abuse. I should *not* have made them believe that our life was normal and conditioned them to live behind the billboard with me.

My out was through another man, a man I met randomly by chance. The attraction and the connection were powerful, mutual and terrifying. 'I don't need to fall in love,' he said to me, his touch burning my skin. I can't say for sure that we ever did fall in love, but our affair opened the door just a crack for me. Oddly, I still carry guilt over this affair, but it was because of this that I found the courage to leave.

But in leaving I stepped from one frying pan into another. Whatever remnants of myself I had left he tore apart with his own brand of control, before texting me that I wasn't worth it and returning to his family.

There was not much left of me by this stage. I went into a safe house and, as neither of my children chose to come with me, I went alone. It took me around six months before I had the courage to open what was left of my heart and be honest about what had happened. I can't even begin to explain the shock and hurt I felt when people turned on *me*. Most people didn't believe me, and my ex's victim status shot through the roof. I thought I had been lonely within my marriage; it was nothing compared to how I felt out of it.

Nothing was ever about me and my suffering. Even when I was diagnosed with a serious illness after the break-up, my ex said, 'As if I don't have enough to deal with, you go and get sick!' Instead of being acknowledged by my family with sympathy and understanding, my suffering was an inconvenience or a strain on others.

I had nowhere to turn. My mother told me that I was lucky that any of my family would even speak to me, and his mother looked at me in total disgust and spat at me that she didn't think I was 'that kind of a person'. The in-betweeners just avoided me so they didn't have to deal with it. My word against his had always terrified me – I mean, everyone loved him, and my past experiences had proven to me that I would not be believed.

I remember their disbelief and anger so strongly I can almost taste the shock and pain in my mouth today. That acrid, dry taste like blood mixed with bleach. Once again, I was not believed. I was dangerously underweight as I had developed bulimia. I had attempted suicide twice and was perpetually like a scared rabbit caught in the headlights of an oncoming car.

***

I am not sure where I drew my strength from to keep going, but I do remember making my entire life source focus solely on my children. Then a woman walked into my life, picked up the broken pieces of me, and started to help me put myself back together. She and her husband became closer than family and incredibly protective of both me and the children. They were like our shield.

These were the first people that I truly opened my heart to and to whom I told my truth. And they believed me. They held my hand through the whole story, and most days it was hard to distinguish whose tears were whose. Together we meditated, took long walks to build up my strength and, most importantly, fought the fight to keep my children with me, where they chose to be. She loved to cook, and everyone sat patiently with me while I forced food down and kept it down, until I was well.

My life became about my children, almost as if I was trying to make up for the years of abuse they had been subjected to. I had my two dear friends, and slowly accepted their friends until I had a tight network. I built my inner strength by being everything I could be to the children. I remember one night hanging up the washing and looking back at the house. There was a soft light from the lamp shining, and the sound of music wafted through on the night breeze. Every now and then the tinkle of the children's laughter could be heard, and I felt a sense of pride – accomplishment even – that all of this was possible because of me.

In looking back, I believe the biggest factor in rediscovering myself was to allow myself time. My counsellor said to me, all those years ago, 'You are like a vase that has shattered into thousands of little pieces. With time, love and forgiveness you will find all those pieces and put yourself back together.'

I have given myself a space where I can be honest about how I feel about my ex. I can remember the gentle soul I fell in love with, as well as acknowledge that we were both already damaged and that our union was the perfect storm waiting to happen. I am working to connect with the young girl suspended in time due to my childhood abuse. I have decided it's time I followed my dream of working hard to be a voice against domestic violence.

Taking life in small bites was the only way that I could live my life. I had financial independence through my job. Being a mother gave me a shield. I learnt to trust myself to love again, letting a man into my life who loves me and my children. In discussing the decision to write this down, my eldest child said to me,

> 'Mum, you can see how amazing you are by just how awesome your children are. We are who we are because of you.'

***

I am sitting on a hill of my choice. Around me lie the remnants of a meal that consisted of all of my most favourite things, especially chocolate. In my hand I hold a glass of wine that I sip from with pleasure. A gentle breeze caresses my face and brings with it the sounds of my favourite kind of music. Shifting in my chair I cross one leg over the other, look out over the valley and sigh.

Exhaling brings forth a gentle calmness from deep in my chest. Breathing in deeply, I search for a pocket of anxiety and can find none, not even the smallest of amounts.

Reaching down, I open the bottle of wine and refill my glass. I don't even check how much I have consumed. I don't care. I'm not going anywhere in a hurry. I pop another chocolate-coated strawberry into my mouth. As I savour the sweet and bitter tastes, I look around me.

In front of me is my life as I now know it. Both of my children are happy, successful and strong. Both of my children are gentle and loving and confident. Both of my children are loved and respected and heard. I am on a study break, my second semester completed and my results a resounding confirmation that I truly can do this, that my dream is reachable.

Hearing the car make its way up the hill behind me, I reach into the esky and pull out a beer for him. Not because I have to, but because I want to. He drops a kiss on the top of my head, takes the beer and opens it.

'Guess you didn't save me any chocolate?'

I smile and shake my head. With a laugh he sits down next to me and together we wordlessly admire the view.

My life without abuse is like this. I am happy and confident. I am driven and outspoken. I am proud and fiercely protective. I have a choice now and I won't take any crap. I am nurtured in a space where I am able to heal and get stronger. There are still hurdles to cross and things to work out, but the life I live now is heaven compared to what I lived in the past.

SHIELD

My journey to sitting on top of the hill, sipping wine, looking at the view and laughing with the love of my life took TIME. I needed to give myself the time and space to heal. What helped was the SHIELD that protected me and my children while we recovered. I will lend you my shield so you too can rebuild your life and make your way to the top of your hill.

Space and support: Give yourself the space and time to heal. Allow others to step in and help you. Ensure you have support from a network of people you trust. Build a new group of supports if you need it, and seek support from a counsellor.

Health: Go for long walks with a friend, practise meditation daily and ensure you eat healthy, nutritious meals with friends.

I believe: The power of confidence starts with knowing that you have a safe place in which to be honest, so that when you fall down, you know someone has your back. I believe the biggest factor in me rediscovering myself was to allow myself time. I believed in me and my children and I believe that you can take this journey.

Employment: Where possible, gain and maintain employment, even a part-time job, as this will help to increase your financial independence and self-confidence, and connect you to another group of people to provide support. Employment will give you more options for the future.

Legal, laughter and love: You may need to take up the fight for your family; get support if you need to go through the legal system. Let laughter into your life and take the time to stop, listen, and hear the laughter that will come. Gradually let love back into your life.

Direction: Take small steps in your new direction toward your freedom. Focus directly on what matters most – you and your children.

© Broken to Brilliant

CHAPTER THREE

WARRIOR

'I am not a victim. I am a warrior.'

'YOU'RE NOT DEPRESSED, YOU'RE JUST A BIT EMOTIONAL,' SHE said as I sat uncomfortably, staring at the well-worn linoleum floor of her room.

Immediately, the smile was back on my face. 'Of course, that's it,' I replied as I adjusted my pants that hid the 'carvings', as I call them, that decorate my thighs.

After gathering so much courage to see my family doctor and ask for help, I was met with rebuttal. If she didn't believe even that smallest detail, she would never believe the suicide attempts. If a doctor would not believe me, no-one would.

And there began the inner war that raged for years: 'I'm fine and it's all in my head' versus 'how could she not see my pain after all these years?'

My GP knew my father! She knew my history! Was I that good an actress? Well, maybe I should give drama a go. Lord only knew I attracted drama in my life like ants to honey.

Intelligent. Smart. Happy. Confident. Those were the words people always used to describe me. But it was all a facade.

But, but, but, if that's what they think, I always have to be happy *for them*. 'That's it! What a fabulous idea,' I thought to myself.

'But why doesn't anyone see me, really see me?' I pondered as I lay in bed most nights, melancholy filling my very being as I thought of people I saw every day who never saw past the mask. And I would succumb to that sweet, dark embrace, wrapping myself in its void as I shrank from the memories that haunted my nights.

***

Growing up in a cult, trusting my gut was the last thing I was ever taught. In fact, it was the antithesis of everything they stood for. Obedience. Subservience. Unquestioning acceptance. For to question was to be impudent. Impudence meant disobedience. Disobedience meant punishment. Punishment meant beatings.

And so, I learnt to accept whatever happened to me. If I was beaten, well, I probably did something to deserve it. And heaven forbid I tell anyone about my father's behaviour – children are meant to be obedient.

This religious dogma became so entrenched in the very fibre of my being that I accepted abuse as normalcy – condoned and even encouraged by God himself – lest I choose death as my preference. For we knew that to leave the good flock was to invite utter ruination and death.

Even though I finally left the cult, 'abuse is acceptable' remained ingrained as a foundational belief within me.

This belief permeated my life to the point where I constantly attracted abusive relationships into my life. I was on a carousel of abuse, hopping off one 'horse' to the next in an attempt to find happiness. If only I had known that all I needed to do was to get off the carousel entirely. Or known that I had the strength to do so.

Having turned my back on the only life I had known, but holding close all the ideals they espoused, I cut off all ties and contact with my primary abuser, only to land straight into the waiting lap of another. 'A romance written in the stars' was not a term my marriage evoked from anyone, but I was so desperate for any sort of love and protection I fell headlong into it, heedless of my gut instinct and the impending danger.

Knowing the oncoming abuse I would experience, and the total loss of control that would accompany it, my father reappeared in my life as if sent by Providence itself. My father was there for me, guiding, helping and supporting me through the endless cycle of psychological abuse from my partner. In the small country town where I was the stranger, my partner was a prominent upstanding man in the community. No-one would have believed the hell I was living. And although my decision to finally break free and leave was the right decision, little did I realise the ulterior motives that lay behind my father's persistent encouragement for me to do so.

Now I was free of my partner, my father could resume control. First came his pleas for forgiveness, unending streams of apologies for being a terrible father and all that he had done. I couldn't help but feel a spark of smug satisfaction to know that he had finally deigned to admit his errors. Then came the plea for financial help due to his divorce proceedings and – what do you know – the old adage that pride precedes a fall was about to ring true for me. Puffing my chest out, I finally knew a pride and joy I had not previously experienced. The man whose love I had always craved finally needed my help ... because he loved me. I was needed and wanted, that small, lost child in me finally receiving the attention she so fiercely desired. I lent him the money.

He was going to pay me back, of course – using the inheritance money my mother had left me, which he had withheld year after year. 'Of course,' I assured myself. 'It all makes sense.'

But most importantly, he was so sorry for everything he had subjected me to. How could I turn my back on that? Forgiveness was the cornerstone of God's love, as I well knew.

'Your father has been arrested.' I could scarcely believe my ears. When I finally spoke to him, he told me how my stepmother had pushed him over the edge and it was she who had driven him to this unspeakable violence, again. Knowing the abuse I suffered at her hands, both directly and indirectly, I immediately absorbed this morsel of information as absolute fact. Every action he had taken up to this day had been either at her behest or due to the stress she was subjecting him to. Absolutely.

'I don't have anywhere to go. Please help me,' came the desperate plea following his eviction. Again I felt needed and loved. I was the only one he could turn to. My new partner begrudgingly accepted this circumstance, though he was weary of my father's behaviours and remained suspicious of his overtures – a suspicion I blatantly ignored.

However, after my father drained our house deposit and savings and left us financially compromised due to reckless business decisions, I finally stood by my partner. And just like that, the curtain lifted. The kindness, the apologies, the self-abasement vanished instantaneously. The physically and verbally abusive tyrant I had grown up with reappeared seamlessly, almost as if it had been itching to be free of the kind-hearted facade. I shrank back inside the shell of the battered child I had used to survive all those years, and my fiance had to force my father from our house.

And so it began.

This time, wiser from his time spent with me as an adult, my father began his manipulative appeals in an attempt to coerce me. For he knew that my desire to be loved was the fuel that could ignite senselessness within me. Here was a man who dreamt, and vocalised, things that should not be said about women – violent sexual fantasies against women, even his own relatives. He was involved in activities that were not aboveboard, and wore it as a badge of honour. Somehow, I had allowed him to convince me that he was the victim and he wasn't really doing 'bad things'. So desperate was I to be loved, so desperate to believe his apologies and forgive, that I was blind to the glaringly obvious truth.

An expert in manipulating me, he began with abusive messages and phone calls that only escalated. Broken, shattered, my faith and heart ripped to shreds, I finally had the strength to go to the police. I was scared they would not believe me or take action, and my worst fears came true – blatant disregard and disinterest in my plight. 'There's nothing we can do,' I heard the police officer say, and I was back in my doctor's room all over again. Muttering some form of thanks, I left the station, my head hanging in shame and rejection.

We drove home, petrified and vigilantly scanning the streets for his car, for we knew he carried knives in his car 'for protection'. We found the front door smashed in, glass littering the floor. Knowing that he had already used 'insufficient evidence' as a way to evade police in prior incidents, I knew it was futile to return to the police station.

And yet I was still not fully convinced of his guilt.

Finally, the moment of enlightenment came, the moment when I was able to crest what was previously insurmountable. I began to receive messages begging me to return to my father, to leave my partner and he would love me again. I finally, forever, recognised the monster for who he was. I would only have his love on his terms, being firmly controlled by him and no other.

The behaviours that I had made various excuses for, or had been convinced were my imagination, were very real. Gagging and endless beatings were not Bible-based, not what God wanted. Being violated and threatened to silence was not Bible-based. And I finally realised this person who was meant to be my protector, my shield, the person I could always turn to and trust – was the complete opposite.

And what had I done? Bile rose up in my throat as the realisation hit me: I'd fallen back into his trap again. I felt both relief at realising I wasn't crazy, and disappointment in myself that I'd allowed him to manipulate me again. The combination created a bittersweet taste in my mouth.

But this time I was smarter. This time I knew his patterns

and tactics, and the perfection with which he could exploit 'the system' with his elaborate stories of self-pity and self-loathing.

I was powerful now. I knew he was not the victim.

My own conceit at believing that I had learnt from my abusive marriage had lulled me into truly believing that I would never again allow abuse into my life. I had never admitted to myself that the most terrorising relationship I had been subject to, was with my own father. And now I knew it.

And I buried it. Just like that.

***

It took almost a year after these events to feel truly shattered. I knew deep down that I was the dregs, the spoilt leftovers, undeserving and never enough, no matter how much I gave and how much I tried. 'You will never be good enough,' was the tape constantly playing. Feeling sick to my stomach, that beautiful, bottomless pit of darkness yawned up at me, desperately trying to swallow me. 'Come back,' came the seductive invitation.

'Never! I am smart, I am independent, I am fearless.' I struggled to resist its pull.

'No, you're not,' came the voice, deep and foreboding, piercing through my very soul and laying bare all I was not. 'You're weak and pathetic and you are never going to be enough. Your parents never loved you, your husband never loved you. You are all alone and you know you are worthless.' The silence stretched as the weight of my ignorance and stupidity hit me so hard, I was physically sick. 'But I won't leave you.' It was always so enticing.

The voices from my past swirled in my head, encompassing my whole body.

Then a different voice, gentle and exasperated. Rough hands gently shook me. 'Snap out of it.'

Looking at me was the man who had stayed by my side. Someone who I never in my wildest dreams would have expected to find true love and friendship with. Steady, firm, gentle. My rock and my mountain. Immovable. He became my beacon in the darkness. And I am so thankful that I have the joy of sharing my life with him now.

Today, I look back and forgive myself. Today, I know that it's okay. Today, I am grateful for the person I have become.

For the last few years, I have had the unwavering support of my partner and also my aunty – a woman who also escaped the cult only to wander into the arms of a violent relationship herself. Her fortitude, strength and determination were qualities that I so keenly desired to emulate but felt too weak to replicate. Through an unending stream of patience and love she showed me I had people who truly cared for me unconditionally. She has become to me a mother, best friend, advisor and confidante, just by letting me be myself and talk without judgement. I felt myself slowly start to trust again, discovering there were people whose motives were pure. And my partner, without whom I would not physically be here, opened up about his own story of family violence. And somehow, as though fate was pulling the strings of destiny, we began to heal together.

Yet, despite this healing I had a hidden rock in my stomach – the dark, heavy weight of anger, resentment and pain that would constantly well up. Then unexpectedly, my partner asked if I would watch the movie *The Secret*. Due to the upbringing I was still struggling to shed, I was sceptical. But I thought, 'What's the worst thing that could happen?' So I watched it.

This was the exact moment my life changed. This was the turning point. Words alone cannot describe the thankfulness I feel for this moment in my life. From this point forward, I opened myself up to self-development, meditation, gratitude and so much more. I cannot begin to explain the depths of self-knowledge this has led me to, along with the exquisite healing power I have been able to experience. Seeing the Law of Attraction work in so many wondrous ways in my life has given me so much happiness, as I strive to further understand this amazing law of the universe.

See, the beautiful thing about opening myself up to the Law of Attraction was that as I laid bare my innermost soul, I clearly saw my own inner blockages. And in recognising them, I gained my power back. I knew what I needed to work on within myself. And how powerful I am because of that.

My life has changed in the most amazing ways. And I want you to find this freedom too. Rather than forgiveness, I learnt acceptance. And in the beauty of accepting and letting go, the hatred fled from my body.

Your mind is the most powerful thing there is. YOU are in control. If you can change your mindset, you can change your world.

Now, this can be as fast or as slow as you need it to be. Our journeys are all unique. Take all the time you need. There are so many things I want to tell you and comfort you with. But mostly

I want you to know that you can take your power back. It all starts with you.

I am not a victim or a survivor. I choose to live every day as a warrior.

For me personally, I needed to let go of my victim mentality to truly breathe as the free soul that I am. For me, calling myself a 'survivor' made me feel as though I was still giving those abusers power over me. We are all different, but this is my story. This is my awakening.

I choose to see the story differently, and with that I experience unencumbered freedom. I do not forgive or justify their abuse, but I see past it. I see their inner child being abused and beaten. I see their inner child desperately trying to comprehend the whys of the injustice. I see their inner child screaming for love. They themselves were perpetuating unbroken cycles of abuse. And so I wish them healing. I want them to be better people so they can be happy. And in that, I gain my power back. For I am in control of my life and how I choose to live it.

Take your power back. Know that you are worthy.

Change your mindset and so change your life.

Appreciation. One of the most important things I have learnt to practise on a daily basis is appreciation. Waking up every morning and just saying, 'Thank you, thank you for this beautiful day', I begin each day with a positive and appreciative spirit and so lay the foundation for the day ahead. Changing the mindset – what a simple but powerful way to focus your attention.

I have been inspired by the Abraham-Hicks teachings that

appreciation and self-love are the most important tools we can nurture.

I am thankful for all I have endured, both the good and the bad. For if I blame my abusers for all the bad that has happened in my life, I must also be thankful for the good that has come from it. Without going through what I have experienced in numerous abusive relationships, I would not be the strong, kind, compassionate person I have become. Thank you that I am alive. Thank you for my drive and passion for life. Thank you for my spirit, for I will never give up. Thank you for my strength, for I can do anything. Thank you for the hard times and the lessons, for they opened my heart and mind to the Law of Attraction.

Being thankful unlocks the door to instant happiness, because the more you are thankful, the happier you become. For when you focus on the good, even if things aren't the way you want them, you will see that there is a world of abundance that is yours!

Meditate. I cannot say this enough. Meditate daily and clear your mind. And just so you know, there is no right or wrong way to meditate. Do what works for you, find what works for you and practise it. Meditation calms and resets our mind, heart and soul for clarity. And from that peace and calmness we can breathe easy.

Feel. Feel your emotions and feel the good. Our mind and emotions work hand in hand once we learn how to utilise these amazing gifts. Envision the life that you want and never lose hold of it, even as it changes. You have an untapped reservoir of strength that you still haven't fully realised because you are so much stronger than your current circumstances. Now that you are starting your journey of healing and discovery, know and feel your amazing life that is to come. Because as you see it, so you will manifest. Because you, my dear reader, are worthy of the best of everything this beautiful world has to offer you. You are worthy. Read that again. You are worthy.

Don't forget, this can take time. It's okay. As Tolstoy reportedly said, 'The two most powerful warriors are patience and time.' Take the time that you need, but never stop, never give in to the darkness. Know this: you are a warrior, your time is now. You are stronger than your past. You are stronger than any challenges that may come. Warriors are built from the struggle, formed from the pain, strengthened by the challenges. Embrace your challenges and push through them like the warrior you are.

Every experience in my life has led me to who I am and where I stand. And that is always the right place to be. I finally have freedom. I can choose my life and what I want from it and in it. I never thought I would be here or that I could be truly happy. I am free. And I can be or do or have anything I want. So can you.

I had let the feeling of worthlessness dictate all the decisions I made, so that my life coalesced into a swirl of negativity and resentment. I resented people who were happy, I resented people who were pursuing their dreams. But mostly, I resented myself for being weak. Now I know that I am worthy.

My final step to becoming a warrior – the moment I fully felt freedom and relief – began as any other day. I had come to realise that my job was the last tie to my feelings of unworthiness, my last blockage. I had allowed myself to be mistreated and bullied, working in a base role, feeling that I could never do any better. Now I knew.

This time, without a tremble or worry in sight, I firmly held that piece of paper. That single piece of paper that marked the new me, the free me. And so I walked in, my resignation in hand.

The smell of the air-freshener they used in that office no longer assaulted my senses but pleasantly lingered on the periphery, no longer a symbol of the bullying I faced. This time I had been weighed, I had been measured, and I had been found worthy. And I experienced the indisputable power of the Law of Attraction working for me, because I held no tortuous indecision. The person who had bullied me was not there, their office empty, and so I gently placed my letter on the desk. Walking away I knew for certain, a private smile lighting my face. I knew my worth.

Who knows what the future holds? Who knows what will happen next? But I am a warrior. I am free and I will conquer the world.

Change your mindset - MANIFEST your freedom

My life has changed in the most amazing ways. And I want you to find this freedom too. Our journeys are all unique. Take all the time you need. I want you to know that you can take your power back. It all starts with you. Change your mindset, to change your life.

Let go of the victim mentality to truly breathe as the free soul that you are. You are not a victim. You are not a survivor. You are a warrior. You thrive!

You are in control of your life and you can choose how to live it. Take your power back. Know that you are worthy.

Your amazing life is to come. Because as you see it, so you will **MANIFEST** it.

Meditate daily: I cannot say this enough. Find what works for you and practise meditation daily. Meditation calms and resets the mind, heart and soul for clarity. And from that peace and calmness we can breathe easy.

Attraction: I have seen the Law of Attraction work in so many wondrous ways in life. It brings much happiness and freedom. So, strive to further understand this amazing law of the universe. From this law, learn acceptance and in the beauty of accepting and letting go, the hatred will flee from your body.

New mindset: Your mind is the most powerful thing there is. YOU are in control. If you can change your mindset, you can change your world. What a simple but powerful way to focus your attention. For when you focus on the good, even if things aren't the way you want them, you will see a world of abundance that is yours.

Inner blockages: With self-reflection, clearly see your inner blockages. Open yourself up and bare your soul. By recognising your inner blockages, you will gain your power back. Know that you will need to work on yourself. You will gain your power back from working on yourself. It all starts with you.

Forgiveness: Today, I look back and forgive myself. Forgiving yourself will set you free. I do not forgive or justify their abuse. I choose to see the story differently, and with that I experience unencumbered freedom. I see past their abuse.

Emotions: Feel your emotions and feel the good. Our mind and emotions work hand in hand once we learn how to utilise these amazing gifts. Envision the life you want, and never lose hold of it even as it changes. Every experience in your life has led you to who you are. And that is always the right place to be.

Secret strength and support: Watching *The Secret* was the exact moment my life changed. This was the turning point. Open yourself up to self-development, explore the depths of knowledge and the healing powers of gratitude, meditation and the power of the universe. You have an untapped reservoir of **strength** that you still haven't fully realised because you are so much stronger than your current circumstances. Gain your **strength** back. For you are in control of your life and choose how you live it. Take your power back. Know that you are worthy. Know that you are a warrior. Warriors are built from the struggle, formed from the pain, **strengthened** by the challenges. Gather unwavering support from family and friends, support that provides an unending stream of patience and love, support that cares for you unconditionally.

Thankful: One of the most important things I have learnt to practise daily is appreciation. Wake up every morning and just say, 'Thank you, thank you for this beautiful day.' Begin each day with a positive and appreciative spirit and so lay the foundation for the day ahead. Being thankful unlocks the door to instant happiness, because the more you are thankful for, the happier you become.

© Broken to Brilliant

CHAPTER FOUR

CHAMPAGNE TASTES

'There are important things in life that the hand cannot touch, the eye cannot see, and money cannot buy. Happiness is achieved through how we perceive the world, and vision, intent and tenacity will help me realise my goals.'

It was a hot summer afternoon and I had just returned from a motorbike ride along my favourite winding beach road. As I walked into the kitchen, I noticed my wife's agitated body language.

I asked her if anything was troubling her. She said no, but I could see the guilt-driven uneasiness in her body language and in her eyes. I looked her in the eye and said, 'You are having an affair, and I will tell you who you are having the affair with.' I said his name, and she replied, 'Yes.' She informed me she was leaving me and taking our two young children with her, to live with a good friend of mine.

She said I was a failure, a 'gunna' – gunna do this, gunna do that. She said the university degree I planned to commence in six weeks' time, in my forties, would also result in failure. She said our entire long-term relationship had been a nightmare.

Then, near the end of being told how she saw me and our life together, she stated, in what appeared to be a sincere tone, 'You will do very well now that I won't be around to hold you back.'

I was confused. In one breath it was my fault I was a failure. In another breath, she was the cause of me being a failure. My negative emotions took control and quickly placed me in deep distress, causing me to think in circles, searching for answers to resolve the situation, answers that would never come to me.

***

I moved back to my childhood home, to live with my widowed mother. I was back in my old bedroom that I had shared as a child with my two younger brothers. My life was now a bedroom with a single bed, small bedside lamp, a second-hand computer I did not know how to use, and a very small bedside table. I had gone full circle, back to my pre-marriage days.

That night, I sat on the edge of the bed pondering how my life had come to that point, and I cried. I had been betrayed by two of the closest people in my life. I had lost everything I had worked hard for and had no money. A student allowance would be my sole source of income for the next four and a half years.

I questioned deeply whether or not I was a failure as I had been told. At 40, was I about to waste time and money going to university?

Just before getting into bed that first night I formed the strong vision of completing my degree. I promised myself that nothing – absolutely nothing – would stop me from doing so. Failing at university was not an option, as it would confirm the claim that I was a failure and a bad example to my children. I had to tenaciously hold onto my positive vision of completing my degree, have rock-solid intent and not allow anything or anyone to stop my vision becoming reality.

Reflecting back to that night full of fear and loneliness, I realise it taught me that to be successful you do not necessarily have to believe you can achieve. Vision, intent and tenacity are what deliver the outcome you work for.

***

As time moved on and university commenced, I reflected back over my marriage and searched for clues. Six months after we were married, I had noticed changes in the way my wife was treating me. She questioned my actions, and put down me and my friends. When I had the opportunity to go into partnership in an extremely successful and lucrative shop owned by a family member, I was told I would fail and that I was not to go ahead. 'You don't know anything about the business. Anyway, the bank will never lend *you* the money.'

Questions continually ran through my mind. 'Have I done the right thing being in this relationship? Should I stay or should I leave? What have I done in this life or a previous life to bring on this treatment of me?'

However, I was trapped. Shortly after we were married we started a family and there was no way I was going to leave an unborn child. If my wife had not been pregnant, I would have left.

Several years before the marriage ended I again contemplated – without reaching a decision – ending the relationship after my two children had finished their education. I experienced what I now know to be the fear of rejection, which has the powerful underlying fear of being unloved. The need to be loved can blind us in many ways – hence the saying 'love is blind'. I was totally emotionally blinded by the fear of being unloved and subsequently endured an emotionally and psychologically damaging marriage. I was not capable of making the decision to leave.

I believe that early in our relationship two insecure attachment styles emerged. For me it was a need for closeness and connectedness, and for her it was a need for distance and space. Those two styles of attachment were a recipe for disaster driven by an underlying fear of rejection.

We met in our mid-twenties. I had not been married before and she had divorced her first husband some years before. She disclosed to me that she had mixed emotions about her previous relationship and feared being 'left on the shelf', as she put it.

The realisation years later that my relationship was based on insecurity had a profound impact on me, and I would not enter into such a relationship again. I also realised that the fear of being unloved can drive people into, and trap them in, damaging relationships, including relationships where one party is heavily controlled by the other.

Consistently, my wife stopped me from doing many things, including going to university. On the first occasion I mentioned that I wanted a university degree, I was met with, 'You don't expect me to work while you study, do you?' It was made plain to me that she was not going back to work, and I had no hope of going to university.

I was heavily controlled. No matter what I did, it was not good enough. I was put down to her family members and in front of our friends. Not earning enough money was a constant criticism, which eventually led to me having to work seven days a week. I was constantly told I had 'champagne tastes on a beer income' and that she 'deserved better'.

It was always being pointed out that I went to a public school whereas she attended a private school. Many times, she said, 'I should be married to a highly-paid professional – a surgeon or a lawyer. Instead, I have a public servant.'

All major financial decisions were made by her. This included who should own a car. If I wanted a vehicle of my own, I had to find the money without it affecting the running of the household, so I borrowed money from my family to buy a small car. The household budget was tightly controlled by her, right down to our individual pocket money.

Her belief was that sex was something you did to please your husband and to have children. Our sex life was almost non-existent, and punctuated with the direction, 'You have five minutes.' Whenever she could, she came to bed after I had fallen asleep. On one occasion after I asked if she would like to make love, she flew into a violent physical rage and drew blood by cutting three long deep grooves into my forearm with her fingernails. That was the last time I made any sexual advance toward her.

Despite that physical assault, I didn't realise I had been living in an abusive relationship until well after I started at university. Abusive relationships were heavily discussed in my degree. I started to see the parallels with my relationship and realised that I had been a victim of abuse.

The control extended to not being allowed to mention my ancestry (fifth generation born in Australia) despite my family coming to Australia in the mid-1800s. Apparently all people with my heritage, including those born in Australia, were the same, and were responsible for world conflicts.

My friends were never good enough even though they were in the legal, medical and accounting professions. I had many good friends, but while I was allowed to socialise with them without her, that did not include inviting them to our home. 'I am not having your bikie mates here,' she said. (Neither my mates nor I belonged to any motorbike-related clubs.) Or, 'I don't think much of his wife.' Subsequently, over time those relationships ceased.

Even today I suspect that I may have been in some form of denial about recognising or accepting that I was a victim of abuse.

***

In a crisis, you will always find out who cares for you. I certainly did. Support from family and friends was outstanding.

My mother was a great support during that time. The advice she and my father had given me as a child was rock-solid and practical, and so it was again in my time of need. She supported me in many ways during those early years of separation, divorce and of course while I was at university. As was her usual behaviour, she accentuated the positive. She said, 'Work hard and do not give up.' It triggered memories of my father telling me, 'Do not tell yourself you cannot do it. Don't underrate yourself.'

My ten-year-old decided not to tolerate any derogatory remarks made about me. My child would often say about my ex-wife's family, 'They say bad things about you and I get upset.'

I said, 'Just ignore it. It doesn't worry me.' However, what I didn't say was that I was concerned about what the comments were doing to both the children.

This eventually came to a head on one occasion when I was being put down and my child interjected, 'That's my father you're talking about,' and left the tea table to eat in their room. My child never ate with them again.

To see the display of such strength at such a young age was inspirational for me in working through my issues. My child continues that support today, as do others.

My best friend at the time questioned me as to whether I was suicidal. He not only showed great concern for my wellbeing, he was always there when needed and regularly checked up on me.

The biggest revelation while at university was the way my fellow students, both male and female, accepted me. This was a major thing for me, especially as we worked so closely together for more than four years. The discussions about life, relationships and academe helped dispel the negativity I had developed during the years of abuse.

My university studies helped me greatly in understanding that I was not mad, useless or bad. That time at university helped me change the way I saw myself and my failed marriage. It also helped me understand my wife's issues and her own painful struggle with them.

***

Just after the first 12 months of separation, I made the decision to let go and get a divorce. For me this was a major positive decision and event: it was me leaving her. My wife had told several friends, 'He will never divorce me as he is emotionally dependent on me, and waiting for me to go back to him.'

Once the divorce became absolute, my wife and I met. I told her I wanted us to free each other from our wedding vows, and we did just that. For me, this meant I had the final say in our marriage and I was now totally free – legally, mentally, emotionally, spiritually, physically and financially.

There were several factors that led me to taking divorce action.

I will never forget a lecture on family violence during my first year at university, which was also my first year of separation. I learnt that emotional, psychological, financial and coercive abuses were also included in the definition of family violence. That lecture was an eye-opener for me. I had never been exposed to family violence growing up, and didn't recognise it up until commencing university. I thought family violence was only physical. I deeply reflected on the years we had been married and how I had been treated. The primary focus was the emotional and psychological abuse – both subtle and blatant – that I had been subjected to.

My academic results at university also caused me to severely challenge my low self-esteem and lack of self-worth that developed during my marriage. Those results were proof that I was not the person my wife said I was. I was asked to do an honours year – a surprise, and also further proof that I was not a failure. I remember thinking to myself, 'All those years where I was held back, and in the first year of university my abilities and achievements are recognised and rewarded. Why did I not go to university earlier?'

During my time of reflection, the effects of that treatment on my self-worth and the development of feelings of inferiority became very evident. This was disturbing to acknowledge.

I will always remember the incredible sense of freedom during the separation, which played a large part in deciding to divorce. That sense of freedom continues to this day, more than 20 years later.

***

I had a strong fear of being alone, unwanted, unloved. I wanted another relationship to feel good.

Early in my separation, I commenced a relationship with a woman nine years younger than I was. That relationship taught me many wonderful things and helped set the foundation of my recovery. This special woman had come into my life for a reason, especially as we both had many déjà vu experiences in relation to each other. One of the greatest things she taught me was that for a relationship to succeed, both parties need to be individual selves, and it is okay if the parties disagree on some issues.

She constantly told me, 'Be yourself. I am not your wife.'

I learnt what a truly connected relationship was, as opposed to a relationship based on insecurity. Here I was, for the first time in a relationship where I could be myself, and she was teaching me how to do so.

I did not fear being disconnected. When she ended the relationship, I didn't feel abandoned, and we parted on good terms.

I was finally free of the delusion of insecurity. I was an independent individual who was able to self-reflect from a learning perspective, not from a self-punishment perspective.

***

A friend of mine who had also left a disastrous marriage was staying with me for a few months. We were sitting under the back verandah of my house, enjoying a cold drink and taking in the view of the surrounding bush. My friend turned to me and said, 'Mate, what you have done since your separation is unbelievably inspiring.'

I replied, 'What do you mean?'

He said, 'You completed a degree with honours, you bought this house, and you have presented at a prestigious conference. How do you do it? You just keep going. How?'

Some years earlier, one of my children had also asked me a similar question. I didn't know how to answer their questions. Up until that time I had not realised my successes.

Several years later I realised that my path was similar to the loneliness of the long-distance runner. Unwittingly I had been telling myself, 'Don't look back and recognise how far you have come. Keep focusing on crossing the finish line – you have a long way to go.' The irony is that my 'beer income' had started to deliver on my 'champagne tastes', and I had not realised it.

Motorbike riding played a big part in my moving forward and is still a big part of my life. It had been a big part of my life from my early teenage years as my father was involved in the motorbike industry. I managed to keep my bike after the separation and rekindled industry friendships.

I developed an interest in using Buddhist philosophy and practices to help me understand my state of consciousness and to help others understand theirs. Pranic Healing, studying Buddhist philosophy, taking the Bodhisattva vow, and meditation were important in my recovery and personal development. This unravelled a lot of the confusion, frustration and anger that I had carried for many years and had no way of resolving.

My interest in researching through reading was rekindled. I explored various interests I had in the past plus new interests that were developing. My mind now had the freedom of an unrestricted openness to expand in both thought and expression that had been suppressed during my abuse.

A friendship with one of my former mates was very important in a number of ways. We were both busy during the week, and decided we would allow ourselves to meet for an informal happy hour or two on a Friday night to wind down the week. We met at a local pub and both found our time together beneficial.

Contact with my two children was very important, and I spent considerable time explaining my university experiences and results to them. It was important to me as a father to show them that when severe adversity hits, a person can concentrate on the positive and still succeed. There was an element of proving that I was not the failure they were told I was. It was also to show them that they could go to university and succeed, even though they had both been told they were not good enough to do so. Both of my children successfully completed their university degrees and now work in their respective fields of study.

***

Rebuilding your life can be very difficult at times. However, when you realise you are truly free it is a lot easier, especially if you have a strong vision of what you want.

Completing my degree was a major accomplishment for me, especially as my study would never have been commenced if I had stayed in the abusive relationship. I now work in a field I am passionate about and find rewarding in many ways. This has allowed me to speak regularly at conferences both here in Australia and overseas.

My social network is the strongest it has ever been. I have new friends in several countries, and have re-established some of my old friendships which had fallen by the wayside. I provide my professional services for free to a sporting club. This is part of my way of giving back to society for the opportunity I was given to complete a university degree – an opportunity I thought I would never have.

Life confronts us with many unexpected challenges, opportunities and meetings. Given my new-found self-confidence and the progress I had made over the years recovering from the abuse, I was now ready for a relationship with someone I was connected with in a number of ways. I wanted a relationship similar to the one I had early in my separation. Was that possible, would I find such a relationship and would it be mutually beneficial to the lady and myself? By sheer chance, I discovered that a friend from the past had been separated from her husband for many years. I had been attracted to this lady more than 25 years ago when I was single. She never knew how I felt about her until we met again, when she said, 'What took you so long to find me?' I answered in a suitably larrikin way, 'I was separated and divorced years before you – you should have found me.' We both laughed, and now continue to enjoy a great life together. I had found the great relationship that would be part of my vision for the future.

***

The beach had always been an important part of my life as a child, and something my own children enjoyed. A week or two after separating from my wife, I went to a favourite beach alone. It was a hot summer morning and I arrived early, one of only a handful of people on a long beach with steep sand dunes, miles away from suburbia.

As I walked into the water, I experienced a great sense of relief and connectedness that could best be described as a state of *equanimity* (calmness and composure, especially in a difficult situation). I realised I was totally free of abuse for the first time since it commenced.

I experienced a clarity of mind and a sense of purpose that still prevails today. It was as if the clouds had parted and I could see the sky and the sun. I remember thinking to myself, 'I may have lost my family, my home and the future I imagined with my children, but I still have my enjoyment of the beach. No-one can take that away from me.'

I also realised that my children were not lost to me. They were very much connected to me. If anything, the relationship would strengthen. (Over time, this did happen.)

Being at the beach by myself was a new experience – pleasant, contemplative and motivational. I realised that my perception

– either pessimistic or optimistic – would play a big part in the outcome of what I did or didn't do.

I didn't know it at the time, but that beach experience would later be the basis for some of my writing about human behaviour. It also reinforced my vision of being successful in whatever I did. A simple act of going to the beach had changed my perspective of what enjoyment was, and no-one would ever take that away from me.

There are important things in life that the hand cannot touch, the eye cannot see, and money cannot buy. My experience at the beach was obviously one of them, and I set out to find others. If happiness is a state of mind achieved through how we perceive the world, then I was about to test and question my perception at a number of levels on a number of things, to find the positives.

I have never forgotten the importance of having vision, intent and tenacity as tools to realise my goals.

Concentrate on the POSITIVE and succeed

Rebuilding your life can be very difficult at times. You will need to work hard and not give up. When severe adversity hits, concentrate on the POSITIVE and you will succeed.

Vision, intent and tenacity have been the tools I have used to realise my goals and achieve my champagne tastes on a beer budget. Follow these POSITIVE steps so you can pop the champagne cork on your new future.

Perception: Your perception, whether pessimistic or optimistic, will play a big part in the outcome of what you do or don't do. There are important things in life that the hand cannot touch, the eye cannot see, and money cannot buy. Focus on what is important to you and be optimistic.

Others: Take the time, energy and the opportunity to give back to others in the community. This will increase your sense of value and self-worth.

Support network: In a crisis, you will always discover who cares for you. Connect with supportive family and friends. Create a strong social network and re-establish some old friendships.

Interests: Develop an interest. I took up Buddhism and took the Bodhisattva vow to practise the six perfections of giving, moral discipline, patience, effort, concentration and wisdom in order to attain enlightenment for the sake of all beings. Having an interest will help you to structure your time, give you purpose, help to build connections and give you a topic to discuss.

Tenacious: Be tenacious. Use the information and learnings from your experiences to improve and rebuild your life. This will mean a change and an improvement in the way you tackle life.

Intent: Have a rock-solid intent not to allow anyone or anything to stop you from achieving your vision and goals.

Vision: Form a strong vision of your completed goals. Make a promise to yourself that absolutely nothing will stop you from achieving your vision.

Equanimity: I found that spending time on the beach and walking into the water provided a great sense of relief and connectedness that could best be described as a state of equanimity. Equanimity is calmness and composure, especially in a difficult situation. I had lost my family, my home, and the future I imagined, but I realised I still had my enjoyment of the beach. No-one could take that away from me. Find what gives you your calmness and composure.

© Broken to Brilliant

CHAPTER FIVE

THE STEPS TO YOUR FUTURE SELF

'I'm not a victim and I'm not a survivor. I'm a prevailer, an optimist. Where trauma resided, hope moved in. I'm brave and I'm beautiful.'

EVERY SO OFTEN I HEAR CRYING. POLICE HOVER IN PACKS. I'M waiting in the seedy corridors outside the family violence rooms. I feel churned up. If I think about it too hard, I will vomit into that bin opposite me. Talking with the police prosecutor, I know I'm blinking too much, distracted, wringing my hands. The security guard is keeping a watchful eye. The Legal Aid worker mingles. The family violence worker is busy.

And we wait.

How have I traversed two legal jurisdictions, surviving more than one hundred court attendances and two trials?

There's lots of tricks. The basics include carrying a tiny vial of lavender oil, hot thermos of liquorice tea and a muesli bar. A LEGO Minifigure resides in my hand. I fiddle constantly with the pendant around my neck – it reminds me that I'm brave and I'm beautiful.

I choose solid shoes, not sandals; he doesn't get to see my toes. My jacket covers me; he can't see my body. My hair remains uncut to form a cloak; my face is hidden. He doesn't deserve the privilege of 'seeing' me. He can't have that.

I'm not a victim and I'm not a survivor. I'm a prevailer, an optimist. Where trauma resided, hope moved in.

***

'Keep your house key, of course,' I said, 'but remember this is not your home anymore so please respect that.' He only needed access to the outbuildings, not the main home.

He continued to run a business from my home after he moved out. Supporting him was not really my choice – he sought my agreement, but the consequences should I have disagreed would have been dire. I felt the familiar pressure to go with the flow and agree.

When he moved out he removed his personal effects. One night I arrived home, turned my bedroom light on, and the hair stood erect on both arms. Items of his clothing lay neatly folded in the cupboard which had remained empty for months.

When I confronted him, he explained that it was *his choice* and he'd be moving back in. He didn't.

Once, he rummaged through the rubbish bin in my bathroom where he retrieved highly personal items. In front of our young child, he presented the items and proceeded to accuse me of having an affair.

He accused me of having an affair because he saw me nicely dressed.

Even though he agreed not to enter the house after he moved out, he would let himself in and inspect the contents of my kitchen sink. If there were two tea cups I would be accused of having an affair so I learnt to only ever leave one. Even if I had consumed two cups of tea, I would wash one and put it away and leave the other one in the sink.

There was never anything between me and 'other men', but I was confronted often with this threat: 'If I ever find out you're seeing someone else, then I'm not going to be happy and you're not going to be happy.'

One night I woke from sleep with a start – he was standing at the foot of my bed staring at me.

The feeling of threat, the prickling skin, the choking feeling and the dense solid mass in my gut. Like one of Pavlov's dogs, I only need to recall these events to feel the trauma again – it infiltrated my DNA.

***

'Mummy, is today when Daddy collects me from school?'

'Yes, sweetheart, it is.' Each week, my former partner collected our child from school.

'Oh no! That's the day Daddy massages my teacher's feet, and I have to wait.'

I was at the bathroom mirror preparing for work. I felt an odd prickling on my arms and turned around to face my child. 'What do you mean?'

'My teacher shuts the classroom door and he massages her feet and shoulders because she hurt her knee.'

I hoped the childlike description was a little skew-whiff. A week later when the teacher asked me if my former partner preferred red wine or white, I immediately knew that my child's story held true.

Shattered to Shining

The following year, he targeted a different teacher, gifting her wine and flowers in the classroom. After beginning the year with genuine regard, warmth and respect for me, she began to treat me as if I was cruel-hearted.

Another teacher who fell for the manipulative stories went on extended leave then resigned. It never took long for this manipulative, charming man to turn around a support network. Charm, humour, flattery and attention were perfect ammunition in his weaponry of destruction.

When I tried to explain, the principal tried hard to understand, but was confused and wondering who to trust. The charmer was good at whipping up crazy confusion, so that people second-guessed what their gut instinct already knew.

In order to understand my absolute confusion, overwhelming isolation and growing despair, I commenced reading. Through books, I was introduced to descriptions of predators and narcissists. I read *him* in those pages.

I came across the 'Hare Psychopathy Checklist'. When I completed the quiz and ticked off 16 of the 20 criteria, I knew I was dealing with something big.

Survivors of a psychopath relationship will warn primarily – above anything else – to trust your gut instinct (intuition, self-talk) and RUN! Carve out a pathway and get away while you can.

***

When we first met, I learnt quickly to avoid him – he would flirt crudely, try to engage me in conversation and ask me out insistently. Having just separated from a committed relationship,

I was sad and alone and living in a new suburb. I was working hard and successful in my career. He pursued me incessantly until I reluctantly gave him my assistant's number.

Next thing I knew he was calling her, explaining he was 'driving past' and 'had time for a quick coffee', insisting till I agreed to meet him. He took me to dinner – always in my car. Later I found out he had borrowed his friend's fashion items to wear and his 'house' in a neighbouring trendy suburb was a rented room.

He lived in deficit, dealt only in cash to avoid tax and didn't pay debts. Society's rules were not his rules.

He regaled me with stories of a crazy ex-fiancée, and I believed him.

He moved into my life. Accessed my mind, my network, my world.

One night I received a threatening phone call and was so frightened for my safety I called the police. The police attended and advised me to leave my home – I wasn't safe there. I was convinced the caller was him because it was the same week he'd suggested he move into my place and I had refused. I guess he believed that, if frightened, I'd run to his arms. I didn't.

Once he moved in, I spent years trying to get him to leave. Preparing for a work trip I left a long letter – one of many – explaining why he must move out while I was away. He was defiant in his claim on my life and stayed.

He regularly pursued and verbally attacked me. He would trap and block me to provoke and ridicule. I eventually collapsed on the floor, curled tightly, arms around my legs to protect myself, because I was unable to get past him. I cried uncontrollably. I'm robust – it took a lot. He appeared to enjoy this. Once I was so undone in this way his demeanour would change completely. He would smile, be loose in his body, and start talking of our next family outing. This happened repeatedly for most of our long relationship, notably during my entire pregnancy.

I discovered his addiction to porn and casual sex. He was meeting women for sex at his workplace. When I confronted him, he laughed, shrugged it off, said it was me with the problem and all men were doing it. I just didn't know because I was so naive.

Friends were starting to disappear and his family was moving in. It was confusing and alarming. My life of success and confidence, amazing networks and achievements was starting to dissipate around me, and I had no idea why.

I just knew I wanted him to leave.

I wanted him to leave every day from the first day I met him. It took many years for him to move out of my bed, and many more before the police stepped in and put an action plan behind their deep concern for my personal safety.

He converted my calm life into a roller-coaster and I never bought a ticket for the ride. He caused confusion – chaos combined with smoke-screening, fear and isolation and loss. Any confidence I previously had evaporated – I was relentlessly under threat, hypervigilant and walking on eggshells. I ceased planning for future events, it was futile. There was usually drama and cancellation – people eventually stopped including us in their lives.

Isolation set in.

***

My child was challenging. Hypervigilance has a way of converting to behavioural disorders in kids.

I lived with the painful reality that, if I stepped in to protect my child, neither of us would fare well. Witnessing my partner yell at our child for not completing menial tasks was traumatic. I felt conflicted, forced to be silent as he manhandled our child into the corner – it didn't matter where we were – the big, towering, angry, volatile monster trying to discipline the defiant toddler. Should our child dare to glance around, they'd be so violently forced back, I wondered if one day I'd have to mutely watch as my child's arm was pulled out of its socket by their daddy.

He threatened our child for years under the guise of discipline: 'If you don't stay in that corner, then I'm not going to be happy and you're not going to be happy …' The open-ended threat was simply terrifying to a creative, articulate, imaginative child.

My child's previously-diagnosed behavioural disorder 'disappeared' not long after our separation. My child's 'miraculous' recovery was attributed to the fact he no longer lived in a home requiring hypervigilance to survive, and this resolved the disorder. *The child's parents had split, and the child was doing better!*

It's not in my nature to have regrets. However, if I allow myself just one, I regret choosing such a poor father for our child.

I often wondered what life would have been like if I had bought the little apartment near the ocean rather than the one that led to me meeting him. Sliding-door thinking, however, is not helpful. So instead I embrace the opportunity to keep moving forward.

I came to understand over time that people whose lives had been impacted by a narcissist/predator became my teachers, friends, supporters and, at the darkest of times, my saviours. This is important because isolation is the jewel in the psychopath's sword. Done well, it can cause the complete and utter devastation of the functioning life you have built.

***

During the days, weeks and months after our separation, he made a point of visiting many of my closest friends. My childhood mate was confronted by him at work and later told me he was 'verbally violent', questioning my friend about my activities and making accusations in front of our child. My friend cautioned me to get far away from him.

It didn't take long for the manipulative charming man to turn around my support network. He was a master at it – the best. Charm, humour, and unexpected attention were perfect ammunition in his weaponry of manipulation.

In the street in which my child and I remained after he moved out, he would appear almost daily. One day he visited three neighbours sharing stories about me that were untrue. Sadly, some believed his manipulative stories and accused me of being cruel. Others had the strength to approach me about his visit and find out the truth.

It seemed usual for people to be manipulated by him – *and believe him* – despite my friendship with them, integrity, family status, neighbourly connections. They'd believe him and evacuate. Ultimately, I was alone.

Every manipulative word and action was crafted to depict himself as my victim, to demean me, to make others lose trust in what they knew of me, and to damage the friendships that I relied upon and from which I derived support.

***

Sex was laboured, with obligation and fear. If I refused him, he became agitated and angry. He would leave the bed and pace angrily up and down the hallway. If I didn't get out of bed to 'see if he was okay', he would be angry with me for that too. I learnt to adapt and adjust my choices, to deflect the constant angst of his angry, aggressive moods.

'Do you want a *cuddle*?' he would say. One night I was in bed early, sick and exhausted after days of illness. Still working, still mothering, still running the household, but in bed early. I was coughing violently from deep within my body and quite ill. 'Do you want a cuddle?' he said, getting into bed. Supressing my incredulity, I said, 'I'm sick, I can't.'

Like a sudden storm building to a typhoon, his reaction was immediate and foul. Pacing the hallway – using the hysterical voice – he said, 'I'm frustrated because I can't have sex.' Devoid of love, devoid of feeling, devoid of care and devoid of passion. His words were full of hatred. I felt violated.

That last summer before he finally moved out was the last time I allowed him to use my body for sex. I woke as he climbed on top of me. Lucidly, I thought, '*It will be over soon, just let him.*' It took every ounce of resolve to resist pushing him off. When everything else is peeled away, in the core of my compliancy was survival. And I was so worn down. *'Like every other time, I'll just get through it.'* But when I realised he had broken our agreement and used no contraception, I felt nauseated and incredulous.

For many years I robustly resisted speaking of his conduct, justifying my choice simply as, 'That's the dad of my child. I never want my child to read about the monster he was. Anyway, it's in the past.' I now know that I am not responsible for the chaotic terror he caused, but I also know that this man will not ever be in the past.

After years of grief resulting in my life as a whole becoming so violated, I had become desensitised to the cruelty of the relationship with this man.

***

My child and I eventually moved away from the tainted neighbourhood. The day we moved into our new home, we lit some incense together. I said, 'Use this incense to let the house know your wishes for it. Go to every room, corner, space and ask the house for what you need from it. Repeat this as a wish over and over – I will do the same.'

My young child nodded and, with incense in hand, blessed our new home with this wish: 'Peaceful and quiet, I hope we have a safe house. Peaceful and quiet, I hope we have a safe house.' Repeated and repeated dozens of times, then finally with incense hovering over their new bed, this wish: 'Peaceful and safe bed.'

Once safe, warm and free in our little cottage, every single act of kindness presented to me in the years after could only have been described by me as *a shocking act*. I felt unworthy of kindness and attention.

Wisdoms and supports presented themselves, seemingly at the exact time I needed them.

There were people who sought me out to tell me their stories: 'I have a cousin/sister/friend ...' It felt like an honour to help them survive.

My barrister, after a day in court, said, 'Pace yourself – this is a marathon, not a sprint.' These words guided me for years.

My solicitor warmly and empathetically offered suggestions to assist with the trauma she was writing about in my legal documentation.

A girlfriend helped me make sense of the difference between how we relate to our former partner and how the kids do: 'We fell in love with them once, the kids didn't – so they will respond differently to manipulation.'

The supportive neighbour who stayed in touch understood what had happened and offered a safe space. Even though my child was not safe to go there for fear of retribution, it comforted us.

My work 'family' supported my journey, covered for me, witnessed my tears and grief and confusion. They walked past my closed door and made do while I prepared days, months and years of legal documentation.

A girlfriend told me to visit the family doctor (GP) 'today' when she could see I was that low.

The domestic violence service taught me the power of being

believed. The starting point is not a verbosity of words but compassion, support and planning.

A stranger prepared a hamper with a hand-penned note, saying she thought about me every week that year as she collected items for the hamper to donate at Christmas. Each time I read the note I cried.

The women in my family spent hours remotely conjuring vibrating white light to protect me in court. A powerful Mother Earth sisterhood. Other family encouraged, coached and supported me as a person and as a parent, and poured me a coffee or whisky when required and on demand.

Adversity is a wise teacher. I've been delivered some valuable lessons like how to harness and focus my energy – physical, emotional, spiritual, intellectual – to survive and prevail.

I've learnt about the comfort derived from feeling safe. I've felt honest daily gratitude in the ordinary, sweet relief from trauma in humour and laughter, and found healing through creativity.

***

How do I parent a child during separation? Google told me in the early days to *never ever* denigrate the other parent because the child takes on criticism of their parent as criticism of self. Through the massive spikes of trauma, I learnt to be self-caring in order to build my own mental, emotional and physical fortitude to take care of my child.

I learnt that all my child needed when returning home from time with dad was acceptance, comfort, time and space. A lavender bath, a favourite meal, an early night, no homework. I was just present as support because our mum-child relationship was so deeply violated by their dad that they were consumed with guilt, anger, fear, trauma and feeling so alone – alone in their difference.

I wrote in my journal:

My child bawls, interrupted with body parts flailing flamboyantly – screaming, crying and kicking the inside of the car simultaneously. ... self-harming ... scratching at skin, face and body, smashing their forehead into the dashboard. It's distressful to witness this potent bawling anger. The drive home from school is seven minutes.

I'm conscious that my child's classmates will go home, have afternoon tea, play, have dinner and go to bed.

My child's skin is blotchy and eyes red. Hands, clothes and hair are filthy. My child is itchy, has big bloated tummy, and seems completely exhausted.

I've already prepared for this. The bed has sunshine-fresh sheets, snuggly toys and the blanket Grandma knitted. There's a stack of new library books to read. We sit together on the floor and build LEGO for hours. My child removes their clothes and asks me to wash them 'because they stink'. The bath is ready. Dinner is prepared. My child cries off and on for up to three hours after each visitation time. Afterwards, my child talks, knowing they can be themselves and be loved anyway. I listen to the rhythmic mantra in my brain 'compassion – compassion – compassion'. Anything else will just cause more hurt when my child is already hurting so deeply.

'Daddy is a liar,' my child said. 'He forces me to say bad things about people.' My child talks about not being liked at school and that their father said, 'Friends won't ever stand by you so the only person you can ever trust is me.' My child felt upset because of insulting things said about friends, things that were 'really mean'.

'Daddy is a good man except he lies a lot and tells me all the time you're evil. If I call you "Mummy" he yells at me. He forces me to call you "stupid" or "cow". I have to agree with him that it would be great if you were beaten up. Daddy wants me to tell people that I wish you were dead. It makes me feel rotten.'

During extreme moments describing this, my child cried and yelled and pulled at their hair and covered their ears – eyes tightly shut – chanting, 'too much talking, too much talking ...'

When calm returned, I gently asked my child to describe 'a good person'.

'Easy'—counting on fingers—'honest, kind, never says bad things about people.'

My child could list the good people they knew, and realised they had a choice to make.

***

When it's impossible to see the end, it helps me to visualise trauma as an island. For survival, it's fundamental to view myself as a tourist to the island. For respite, I bob in the ocean regularly. One day I will leave the island.

Building a bridge over the quagmire of trauma helped me survive, through ground-based play together – where we play on the floor so that the earth literally grounds us as we talk – and self-care, compassion, quiet. Inside the boundaries of the trauma – which is big and loud and consuming – none of the healing can take place.

Most powerfully and, as it turns out, fundamental to my

survival I began an organic process of visualising a different future. A future free of the legal system, free of hiding and pressure. A future with love and freedom. A future in which my child is happy and well-adjusted, achieving their dreams.

A future where the turmoil inside of me – the silo of rigidity from my solar plexus to my gut and the choking feeling in my neck – has dissolved, and I can frame my past as a gift. Where the wisdom derived has assisted me to reframe the trivialities in life and sort out the people who are true. It helps me know who I am and believe there's something worthwhile to live for.

As my confidence grows I dare to imagine more, and a colourful vision with detail emerges. Imagining, after all, is the first step to making it real.

I imagine a future in which:
- my relationships are my own, untainted by his commentary
- my life is mine, unclaimed by him as credited to him
- my actions as parent are never used as material in the legal system to denigrate me as parent
- I am free to decide what is best for my child without court orders that require agreement from my child's father and which exert power and control and deny my child basic human rights like access to health care
- my child's school life is unencumbered by legal threats and trauma relating to confusing or conflicting demands
- I am free to drive/walk/be anywhere without the fear of seeing him

- my child has processed what happened and their anger is replaced with calm, freedom and purpose
- the lies about me are viewed as the mutterings of a crazy man by his ever-diminishing audience
- I'm free to have a romantic relationship without the weight of certain retribution
- my new partner will be the man my child needs to restore trust in relationships so my child, too, can have a great relationship in the future
- I can cut my hair off completely, because I don't need to use it anymore to shield my face. I no longer need to make myself invisible.

***

So tired of the rigid pole of trauma residing down the middle of my body from neck to navel, I decided to get started on my future! I'm in charge of my body and I decided to turn myself into a runner. Having not been a runner before and feeling heavy – in troubles, not kilos – I intuitively knew I must take steps to *literally* move forward.

I commenced. Feeling slightly ridiculous and very self-conscious, I bought some good shoes, found an isolated walking track, and just got started.

I registered myself for a running event in six months' time.

Each step forward, I visualised life in that imagined future.

At the highest arc of the bridge over the freeway, I looked left to the past and right toward the future. With cars whizzing below me I imagined drivers looking up toward me with envy, thinking, 'I wish I was running like she is – free.'

Step by step, I converted myself into a runner.

And at the dawn of my first official run, I photographed myself. My eyes wide open, expectant, clear, excited, anticipating success. Looking at that photo later, I saw something I didn't recognise – it was confidence. I was there alone, by choice. Because this was a private journey, it needed no more commentary than it already had – my own.

The following day on waking, my inner voice announced, 'I'm a runner now!' Taking charge of my body, I made a commitment to myself. Incredibly, I didn't break that commitment. I made myself a priority.

Shoes laced, I took that first step and commenced running toward my future self.

The STEPS to your future self

Rebuilding your life after domestic violence is a journey and we each have our own private journey to run. I intuitively knew I must take steps to *literally* move forward. I started with a plan. I made a commitment to myself and I didn't break that commitment. I made myself a priority.

To step forward, first visualise your life and imagine the future you wish to have. Make yourself a priority in your vision.

These are the five STEPS I took to gain freedom. By following these steps you will have commenced moving forward toward the future you have imagined for yourself.

Support: Allow family and friends to provide support, to sit with you, to focus on your safety, to coach you as a person and parent, to comfort you during your times of need. You are not alone.

Trust in your future: Visualise a future beyond the violence. I visualised a future free of the legal system, of hiding and of pressure, a future with love and freedom. A future in which your children are happy and well-adjusted, achieving their dreams. Allow time to visualise the life you dream of.

Emancipate yourself: Set yourself free and choose to be in charge of your body. I turned myself into a runner because I intuitively knew I must *literally* take steps to move forward. It's important to commence. Set goals to support your journey. I registered myself for a running event six months in the future. You can get started too.

Place a wish: We wished for a peaceful, quiet, safe home and bed. Think about wishes; they are different to goals, take steps to materialise them. If you choose, use some incense – in a way, it affirms your intention.

Self-care: Like when the airline steward instructs you to place the oxygen mask on yourself before you assist others, learn what it means to take care of yourself. I learnt that if I took care of myself then I had an essential reservoir of mental, emotional and physical fortitude. Good luck!

CHAPTER SIX

YOUR NEW LIFE IS WITHIN YOUR GRASP

'Take off your armour, open your soul – be You! You have been hiding for too long, let yourself out to see the world. Set yourself free!'

Milk splattered onto the kitchen table. I felt the tension in the house rise, the sound of us holding the sharp intake of breath we were too scared to let out. 'It's okay,' I said to my child. Ironically, that phrase was always the instrument that beckoned the storm.

The howl of his screams followed, evil hanging in the air. The children froze to the spot, too scared to move. I tried to get us to safety as he continued screaming.

He finally retreated to our bedroom. The fear within me when he yelled at me to come in. Step by hesitant step, I walked in, wondering whether this would finally be the night that he hit me. He came close. His hand came up and I wondered how the hell I would get all four of us out.

But my husband knew me too well. He knew I had been abandoned by my father as a child and how scared I was about being left by anyone I was attached to. He had a far better punishment than a beating that would heal in a week or two. He wanted something that would be etched into my soul.

So he got into the car and left the house, leaving me alone for hours – humiliated and broken, lying on my bed bawling my eyes out, feeling like in that moment I would never be able to get up again. My children were distraught – screaming and crying and looking to me for comfort – and I was useless. I cried uncontrollably, unable to fathom how I had ended up in this position.

***

This scene played out constantly in our marriage, at least four or five times a week. It was always my fault and it didn't matter how much I thought I had done to stop him from losing it, there would always be something I had forgotten – the air conditioner on, the screen door left open, the children fighting with each other. There were times when he asked what we were having for dinner and, if I didn't reply with what he wanted, all hell would break loose.

I lived in fear of these situations. Not only was I terrified that the police would be called and my children taken away, but I was also so embarrassed. I felt like the way he treated us was my fault.

I walked on eggshells, anticipating his every move, waiting for the screaming, the swearing, the punching of holes in walls, or the car being used as a weapon to frighten us. I became a shell of a person. My only purpose was to anticipate his moods and try to keep my children quiet so they would be safe.

I had married someone who apparently loved God – who

went to church each Sunday. I thought he was my saviour; instead he was the devil in disguise.

Like a viper waiting to strike, he would cut me down using my deepest shame as his weapon – to annihilate my worth, my sense of belonging and my ability to have faith in myself. This is how he was able to disguise as love and stability in my mind a relationship full of turbulence. This is something he was so practised at, it was a work of art. I have no doubt he lived to perfect it over the years.

Until one day divine guidance stepped in, and neither of us realised it was the beginning of the end.

I was driving home from my children's swimming carnival when I turned on the radio. As I listened, my heart dropped into my stomach. My face flushed and panic gripped my soul as the woman on the radio talked about her domestic violence journey. Gerard Baden-Clay had just been convicted of killing his wife – and the media was awash with domestic violence.

In a single second my armour of denial had been unceremoniously stripped away without my permission. Violated, betrayed and terrified, I wasn't ready for this information and I certainly didn't want this black hole that I couldn't navigate. I fought to move from the black hole back into my fairytale land of love, companionship and happy families. Anxiety continued to grip me as I flew down the rabbit hole. I turned the radio off and pushed the fear of reality deep down inside.

It was too late – what had been heard could not be unheard. I drove for hours with music blasting between my ears until I was able to slip the mask back on and step back into my fairytale world – and hope against hope that I was completely wrong.

My mask and my fairytale world stayed in place for another 18 months, when once again I was ripped out of it – without my permission – and made to face my reality. Only this time I was ready.

***

It was Friday, and I had just finished my grocery shopping when I was again sucked into the vortex of money worries and how it was all my fault. I was just about at breaking point with my husband, though I would never have admitted that. I was on autopilot as I walked down the ramp, when a voice interrupted my spiral into anxiety.

'Excuse me, Ma'am, may I take your trolley to the car for you?' the security guard asked.

My sense of faith and Jesus in this world comes from other people. I am constantly amazed at the generosity and love shown by complete strangers. It is in these moments that I believe Jesus works through all of us.

The cogs in my brain stopped and the fog lifted. The absence of peace engulfed my spirit and all I could do was nod. As I followed behind this man all I could think was, 'What am I doing? I could have this type of respect all the time; I should have this respect.' My unnamed angel walked me to my car, then left as quickly as he came – although not without changing me forever.

At that moment my Energizer Bunny-friend rang. She was ringing to see when I wanted to get my eyebrows waxed. The shame I had spent ten years trying to hide poured out of my soul

– and finally into words that made it all real. My beautiful friend listened in disbelief. Her response was so simple, but it changed the direction of my life forever. 'Do you want to leave him? I'll help you.'

'Yes,' was my reply. It was time. I was so scared, but the pain of staying where I was had now become worse than chancing the unknown. And so began my adventure into the ocean and away from the shore.

The month that followed was hell on earth; we were practically homeless. I had three children to feed, clothe and keep warm. I had hardly any money and I was grieving the loss of my fairytale world. I was at rock bottom. However, every time I thought we were done for, something happened – and I knew God was working through these beautiful people.

The guidance counsellor at the children's school was just phenomenal. She asked me at the very beginning if I needed her to go on the journey with me, and I so did. She never once let me down. I would meet her in the morning after dropping the kids to school and pour my heart and soul out to her as she made me coffee and endless to-do lists for the day. She was my rock and I was in desperate need of that. I was at a point where I had very few people I called friends – because I had been so isolated and made to feel like I wasn't enough. I wouldn't dare tell people what was going on for fear they would think it was my fault – or worse, that I was making it up.

My children and I ended up renting a unit after I begged and pleaded with the property manager to give us a go. I got extremely lucky that she was a survivor of domestic violence and went in to bat for me with the owner. I was absolutely over the moon when I found out our application had been accepted.

I collected the keys from the agency and went to move in while the children were at school. I was feeling pretty good. We now had a home; it should have been all downhill from here.

I remember, like it was yesterday, putting the key in the lock and turning the handle and looking at the unit. The old carpet, the chipped paint, the old appliances.

The reality of my situation fell on me like a ton of bricks. I stood in the middle of the lounge room, tears running down my face that soon turned into sobs and screams. I was terrified – I had no-one. I was in this run-down unit all by myself and somehow I had thought this would be a good thing.

At that moment, I wanted desperately to give up. It all seemed way too hard. I was so ashamed. I had no idea how I got there but I was sure it was my fault. My mind went to my children – what would happen to them if I gave up? How would I explain it to them?

Suddenly the fog cleared from my head. I dried my tears as I slowly gained my footing and stood up. I felt the old dirty carpet under my feet. I looked around again at the worn-out paint, the worn-out appliances and the worn-out me. In that very moment I realised that, yes, we were all worn out, but we still had life in us and I wasn't going to let him win.

He had taken so much from my children and me. He took our right to feel safe away from us without a second thought. I was not going to let him take it anymore. In that moment I made a promise to myself that changed our journey forever. I would get up and I would keep showing up until I had rebuilt our life. He was never going to keep me down again.

I was determined, I was ready, and I was impatient. I wanted it all yesterday. I was happy to put in the hard yards – I just wanted them to go quickly. Unfortunately for me, that's just not how this journey goes. Blood, sweat, and tears – and lots of time – were the only things that were happening. It was painful.

My children and I sang the lyrics to *Keep On Movin'* in the car. 'I know, kids,' I said, 'I know that this is crap and not what we are used to, but I promise you if you just get on the boat with me, I will get us to shore.' What we had wasn't much, but it was okay. I desperately tried to get them to understand that yes, we were going through awful times, but we would come through it. They just needed to trust me.

And they did. They put all their trust in me, and we began to rebuild our lives. That song became our theme song. Every time it played on the radio, we would turn it up and sing at the top of our lungs – and I would silently pray that I could do this.

***

We decided as a family that we would start attending church again. I was petrified about what people would think of me. A single mother with three kids. The questions I would be asked; the judgement. I almost didn't take the kids. However, there were some beautiful people from a church-based domestic violence support service that helped us move and they encouraged me to come back. I was blown away by the support and love that was shown to my children and me then, and still to this day. The church continues to love and support us.

Regaining my faith was instrumental in beginning to thrive. It gave me a solid base to start again, with faith and hope that it would somehow work out.

However, one of the biggest milestones in my journey was going back to work. I had no idea how I was going to juggle everything. I wasn't even sure if I could. But I knew that I had made a promise to the children and I was going to keep it.

For the first few weeks I was petrified just to walk into the lunch room. I was timid – I thought I wasn't good enough and everyone would see what a fraud I was. The thoughts in my head would beat like a drum, repeating themselves over and over again.

I knew I couldn't keep this up. I found a psychologist who had a lot of experience in domestic violence and began going weekly.

After a few months I started to become more confident and looked for ways I could improve my appearance. That's when I decided I had a goal: to run 10 km in a marathon. So every morning before work I laced up my running shoes and I ran. It felt amazing. I felt free as the wind blew against my hair – like nothing could stop me. Over the course of the year I lost 35 kg; I felt like a million dollars.

Other people thought so too. As I dropped my kids off for their supervised visit with their father, he stopped me. The intake of my breath must have been noticeable as I stood in front of him, wondering what the hell he could want. Fear began to move from my heart into my head. I pushed it down, grounded myself by planting my feet firmly on the floor, and said, 'Yes?'

'You look amazing. Whatever you are doing is working,' he said.

The smile crept over my face, the twinkle into my eye – I'd been waiting for this. 'Too bad you'll never have this again,' I said. I turned around and walked out the door leaving him standing there stunned. I was no longer the woman he knew. I was my own person and I would not let him intimidate me anymore.

***

Looking back on the journey, my biggest regrets are how long it took me to realise I needed to leave, and that I didn't recognise the red flags sooner.

We were walking back from church; I'd been dating him for about two weeks. Suddenly out of nowhere we reached my front gate. Entranced in him and the conversation that was flowing between us, I was again lost in him. The rain began to fall on us out of nowhere, as if we were in a movie. He leant down, looked into my eyes and said, 'I love you,' then kissed me passionately.

I was torn. On one hand, this was all I had ever longed for, but the other part of me knew that he couldn't possibly love me in two weeks. He didn't know me. However, I was longing for love, I was yearning for it, and so I pushed my inner voice down and simply believed all the lies he fed me.

I know now that this was the love bombing and idealisation period. It was never going to last. Its purpose was to suck me in to the point where he could devalue me and abuse me. I would have saved myself so much heartache if I had realised this.

However, I don't think I would change history. I look at the person I have become and am still becoming. My relationship with him has helped me to grow and heal childhood traumas that may never have healed otherwise. Surely there would have been easier ways to grow profoundly. However, the strength and faith I have found through this challenge has taught me so much about myself.

As I discovered myself – my strengths and weaknesses – my love for myself increased. I realised that his behaviour had nothing to do with me. I started to see him for who he was: someone who was so full of self-hatred and self-loathing that he couldn't have any hope of loving me – because his own hatred poured out of him and spilled onto everyone around him.

It is because of that understanding that I can now look back and remember with fondness some of the good aspects of our relationship. I hold these memories dear and look at my husband with forgiveness and compassion, and hope that one day God will reach him in his life and help him change.

Going through something like domestic violence tears your whole world apart. When you finally leave, you have no idea who you are anymore. I have learnt so much, both through my time in the relationship and also in the 18 months I've been out of it. I had to rebuild who I was, which was unbelievably difficult. It has taken me a long time and I'm still learning who I am and what I love about myself. But I'm getting there, step by step.

The courage and persistence I found in my own abilities and values blew me away. In a time when everyone thought I would fail, I kept getting up, showing up and ultimately achieving. My love for life and my courage to take risks are helping me rebuild my life and make connections with people I never thought possible.

***

The wind is on my back. Lush green grass, trees in bloom, and beautiful blue sky surround me. The universe conspires for my moment to emerge from my cocoon.

The older, more fragile bodies of my teammates made me see our chances were slim. We were the underdogs, but that seemed like a brilliant act of fate.

The game started. I was like a well-oiled machine. I stared the ball down, grabbed it with both hands like my entire world depended on it. Slosh, slosh, slosh through the dew on the grass, I ran my heart out.

We were ahead. Victory was on the horizon. But at that moment, victory merged with failure. I glanced at our competitors high-fiving and cheering. The urge to be on the winning team was immensely clear in my heart and soul.

My thoughts lifted out of my body and quietly observed from a bird's eye view. This wasn't just a game of tunnel ball. This was me taking off my armour, opening my soul and allowing myself to be truly me with people I had only known for a weekend. The highly-competitive, take-no-prisoners, get-stuff-done version of me.

She had been hiding for so long, scared to let the world see her in full flight. Only now she was free.

Your new life is within your GRASP

It has taken me a long time and I'm still learning who I am and what I love about myself. But I'm getting there, step by step. With courage and persistence, I found my own abilities and values, which blew me away. In a time when everyone thought I would fail, I kept getting up, showing up and ultimately achieving. My love for life and my courage to take risks helped me rebuild my life and make connections with people I never thought possible.

It takes a long time, but just take it step by step. Open your soul – Be You. You have been hiding for too long, let yourself out to see the world – set yourself free!

Remove your armour and emerge from your cocoon. Your new life is within your GRASP.

Goals: Set yourself a goal and go for it. I decided to run in an event and started running. Every morning before work I would lace up my running shoes and I would run. It felt amazing – I felt free as the wind blew against my hair, like nothing could stop me. Choose your exercise goal and exercise daily.

Recognise the red flags: Red flags include wanting to move too quickly into the relationship, saying they love you within weeks. You feel like you are walking on eggshells. Rages when they are out of control with you but can maintain composure around others.

Armour: Remove your armour of denial. Listen to the truth of your situation. Open your soul, allow your true self to shine through. Be yourself with other people. Be You – Be Free!

Support: Seek support. It may be through the school guidance counsellor, a psychologist with experience in domestic violence and/or a church. You will need someone to go on this journey with you, someone who will never let you down. Someone to pour your heart out to and be your rock.

Persistence: Keep getting up, showing up and ultimately achieving. Love your life and have courage to take risks. This will help you to rebuild your life.

© Broken to Brilliant

CHAPTER SEVEN

BELIEVING IN MYSELF

'Reflecting back, I'm immensely grateful for the Higher Power/Universe/God – whoever or whatever it was that was guiding me through those horrific years.'

It was the middle of the night when I was woken by a frightening scream from Mum. Dad was beating her up again. She grabbed me and my sibling out of our beds and ran to our neighbours for safety.

The only place we could hide was in their wardrobe. It was so dark, and the smell was awful. A mix of mothballs and the cigarette smoke on their clothes.

Dad barged his way into their house, and I could hear him yelling, 'Where are they?'

Our neighbour said, 'I don't know what you're talking about.'

My body shook with fear. His heavy footsteps on the lino floor told me he was getting closer. I tried not to breathe loudly, so he wouldn't find us.

I held my breath so hard as he came into the room. He was so close to the cupboard. It was only a moment, but it felt like forever.

Thank God, the neighbour told him off and he turned around and walked out of the house. I almost cried out in relief that he hadn't found us.

Returning home later, we soon realised he had locked the doors. I was the eldest, so Mum got me to climb through the lounge room window to open the back door. I was petrified. Was he asleep or awake?

Once inside, I could see a chair near the back door. He had placed glasses along the top of the chair – a secret 'alarm' to let him know if we returned. I told Mum, who was still outside. She said, 'Go to the front door instead.' It was beyond frightening. What if he was on the other side of the wall, waiting? I was so scared but, being a brave little girl, I did it, as I needed my mummy.

For most of my life, I've had nightmares that someone was coming out of my wardrobe, and haven't connected it to that memory till now.

***

In my early teens, we moved to a safe house. We didn't have any of our possessions or any money, but there was no fighting. Peace at last!

Until he threatened a family member, who gave him our location.

He wrote Mum a letter with empty promises of how he would change, he would get help. In that moment, though only a young teenager, I just knew it wasn't going to change. I begged Mum not to go back – he was terrifying and couldn't be trusted.

We did go back, and just as I'd predicted, it got worse. Not long after our return, I heard Mum screaming. I found her in the backyard, down on the ground as Dad kicked into her with his steelcapped boots.

A neighbour and his mates were watching him. I pleaded with them. 'Stop him!' They just stood there and ignored me.

I felt so helpless. I was just a teenager with no power to stop him. There was no way I could stay and watch, so I went back upstairs. When he walked into the house, I grabbed an old carpet sweeper as my only protection. I found my voice. 'Don't come near me or I'll get the cops to charge your sorry a___.'

Unfortunately, there would be many more incidents where I would have to stand up to him.

***

Living in this cycle of terror had a significant impact on my life, with feelings of unworthiness, fight-or-flight reactions, people pleasing, issues with emotional regulation, sex and alcohol, and never feeling like I belonged anywhere.

My whole childhood was about trying to survive. Mum would get us into bed early so we would be asleep when Dad got home.

He would come home drunk and begin arguing with Mum. As soon as the Neil Diamond music went on, I'd be waiting to hear Mum's bloodcurdling screams as he either beat her up or sexually assaulted her, or both.

To this day, I can't listen to Neil Diamond, especially *Sweet Caroline*.

***

In my late teens, life was a roller-coaster. During the day, I went to business school. Upon returning home in the afternoons, it was back to the scary dips and turns.

For years, Mum drifted in, being our 'mother' – nurturing and caring and protective. Other times, like the flick of a switch, she would join him in alcohol abuse as a coping mechanism. She would take care of the house, but she was emotionally disconnected.

I had a recurring thought pattern of imagining life without Dad in it. How perfect it would be to have peace and not have to stay awake every night and be ready to play rescuer. I thought, *The only way this is going to end is to put an end to his violence.* Every time I stood in the kitchen wiping up the dishes and my hands were on the carving knives, I'd tell myself, 'He's not worth going to jail over.'

***

I also had sexual abuse added to the mix. As a young child the grubby hands of a person attending our home molested me, unnoticed by my mother. Another time, he tried to kiss me in my bedroom, and I ran to Mum. She contacted the authorities, but nothing transpired.

I saw him on my way home from school one day, watching me walk past. I froze for what felt like the longest moment. I then ran and ran, and didn't stop until I got home, breathless.

Unfortunately, that was not the last time I was seen as easy prey. At 16, I'd been going out with a boyfriend for 18 months. One night after my parents came home from the pub, plastered drunk, my boyfriend decided that he didn't want to wait any longer for me to be ready to have sex.

He kept pestering me to drink wine, even though I kept saying, 'No, I don't want to!' He held the glass to my mouth and forced me to drink. My stomach churned and I fought the urge to be sick. The taste was horrible – sickly-sweet. It wasn't long before I felt dizzy.

With my dad 'asleep' on the floor, Mum in bed, and my sibling coming in and out of the room, my boyfriend raped me. I tried to push him off, but he was stronger. I kept saying no. I kept telling him, 'Get off me.' My mind was fuzzy and I kept thinking, 'Why won't he listen?' I kept looking to the floor, wondering if Dad was awake or asleep.

After he finished, I got up and staggered down the hallway to the toilet and vomited. After that, sex became a 'must' every night he came over.

About 18 months after that horrible night, I was at the pub with my family when a much older guy started talking to me. Dad ended up inviting him back to our house. The man told my dad, 'She flashed her underwear at me.' It was a complete lie!

That's when my dad said to me, 'Get undressed and join us.' I refused. He yelled, 'Get undressed or get out of the house!'

So I left. He shut the door and locked it behind me. I have no idea what happened upstairs – all I know is that I spent the rest of the night under the house.

For years, I wondered if Dad was secretly awake on the horrible night I was raped by my boyfriend. I had always felt his eyes on me, like he was perving. Recently, I asked Mum about it. She said she had spoken to him about watching me. 'I reminded him that you are his daughter.'

I instantly felt overwhelming validation. The suspicions I had were real.

Then a sick feeling mixed with anger rose up from the pit of my stomach. He was meant to protect me from harm, not cause it!

***

When I reached 18, I knew I had to leave even though I didn't want to leave my mother or my siblings. I ended my relationship with my boyfriend and, a week later, I found a flat to share close by. I was out of there!

I wish I could say that's when my life turned around. Unfortunately, it would take many years for that to happen.

It was the beginning of a rough, crazy, self-destructive ride of alcohol abuse and total sexual disconnection. Being an extremely traumatised young woman, I developed my own coping mechanisms.

I woke up at a party once, realising several people had been having sex with me while I was passed out. I put it down to being 'wasted'. I also kind of saw it as being normal, even though it didn't sit well with me.

I had so much shame from that experience. However, I now realise this was sexual assault.

Reflecting back, I'm immensely grateful for the Higher Power/Universe/God – whoever or whatever it was – that was guiding me through those horrific years. I'm astounded at the fact that I've survived! That I'm even here sharing my story with you.

Through my healing journey, I've been able to connect with the person I was back then after years of burying her – and all the traumatic events she experienced – deep down in the pit of 'Can't Go There' where shame resided. The belief that I was less of a person because of the things I had done to survive, has been replaced with grief. A grief that I had lost those years of my younger self while having to survive something so horrendous.

The only 'help' I got back then – if you can call it help – was from a guidance teacher who said, 'You're better off getting a job than staying here at high school.'

I thought, 'Oh, okay, obviously I'm not good enough to be at school.'

I grew up feeling so scared of making the wrong move, saying the wrong thing, someone finding out the truth of who I was, what my family was like. I couldn't let people know – what would they think of me? I didn't know how to talk about it. I just kept doing what I knew how to do – sex, alcohol, and keeping people at bay.

***

As a teenager, I fantasised about meeting someone who would protect me from harm, and tell me that it's going to be okay. I started going out to clubs and was being drawn to men who had a mysterious persona.

Friends persuaded me to go out one night, and it was like lightning had struck. He was tall with dark hair, and I could tell by his tight-fitting clothes that he was fit. The eye contact was intense – he had the most piercing blue eyes. I was hooked! He would later become my husband.

A few months later, I moved interstate to be with him. As a result of his work taking him away from home on a regular basis, we had a honeymoon period every time he returned – drinking and sex. He would go to work during the day, but at night it was back to drinking and sex.

On the plus side, when he wasn't there I had peace and freedom. On the downside, I had no friends or family to spend time with. He wasn't into socialising when he was home and, therefore, I never established any friendships.

The change in our relationship happened subtly. He wasn't physically violent. It was emotional and verbal, mixed in with manipulation. Little comments here and there. 'Gee, your a__ is big.' 'You look better without make-up.' 'Are you wearing that?'

Over time it became more apparent, but he kept telling me, 'You're the one with the issues.'

I would tell myself, 'Be quiet, don't argue.' But he just wouldn't let up, and I would fight back. When I did retaliate, by throwing items at him or yelling, he would say, 'See, you're just like your family.'

He belittled my intelligence. 'What would you know? You didn't even complete high school.' He'd ask me mathematical sums to see if I knew the answer.

I thought if I tried to be the person he wanted me to be, then he would be happy.

One day we were driving back from the shops and he dropped a bombshell: 'I didn't think I would marry someone like you.' I didn't want to ask for an explanation but thought maybe he might say something nice. He went on to explain, 'I thought I would marry someone who was petite, educated and career-minded.'

My heart sank. I looked out the window, trying not to cry.

I found the internal struggle tiring. He was great at convincing me that I was the one with the 'issues', but an internal voice kept saying, 'No, it's only because you're standing up for yourself.'

So, after many years of trying to fit into being his 'ideal wife', I found the courage to leave the relationship.

I was now a single parent experiencing emotional and financial abuse from him. This led me back into old coping mechanisms. I began drinking and finding myself in circumstances I didn't want to be in.

***

About three years later, I decided to focus on what I wanted out of my life. I didn't want history to keep repeating itself.

I'd worked in the community sector and gained knowledge around mental health issues as well as having my own lived experience. I decided to change the direction of my career and study.

It was challenging at first, wondering, 'Am I good enough?'

I was drawn to self-help books, such as John Bradshaw's *Healing the Shame That Binds You*. I sought places that had a nurturing vibe to them, so I could immerse myself. When the internet came onto the scene it really widened my sources of information. I sought articles on healing, childhood domestic violence and narcissism.

One of the major shifts in my life was trusting someone to support me to peel the layers back and unpack all the trauma. I've had several counsellors throughout the years. Some got me to a place where I needed to be, and others were not such a good fit.

With my current therapist I've done the deepest inner work. I'll be forever grateful for her coming into my life. She validated all the trauma I had experienced and gave me the safety to start acknowledging the impact of not only the childhood domestic violence, but also to connect with the sexual disconnection I'd been experiencing.

I created a vision board and listened to TED Talks. I watched YouTube clips of people who had been working through their own life 'junk' – people like Mel Robbins, Glennon Doyle and Brené Brown, just to name a few. Honestly, I wouldn't be here right now and able to share my story with you if I hadn't tapped into those tools.

I've also discovered that I'm a warrior who can work through any obstacle in her path with an incredible amount of inner strength and determination. That although I'm not yet comfortable in my own skin from years of shame, I'm getting there. That where once I prided myself on the ability to compartmentalise my fractured life, this is now replaced with a deep sense of knowing that I don't need that kind of toxicity anymore and can now remove those fractured pieces.

I once thought I needed a man in my life to protect me and shower me with love. Through self-discovery, I realised I just needed to see that I've been the one protecting myself all these years. Self-love is way more intoxicating than ending up in a toxic relationship, anyway.

It wasn't easy remaining hopeful, and there have definitely been moments where I nearly gave in to the darkness. Nevertheless, as a warrior does, I fought like hell to uncover my truth, to see who I really am and to embrace the journey of self-discovery. I kept reminding myself I was doing this not only for myself, but also for my children – to break the cycle of toxic relationships.

I'm a spiritual seeker and I stand strong in my truth, transforming my life from one of 'surviving' to one of inspiring others to embrace their vulnerability. I've learnt to quieten my mind and look within my heart and soul and be honest with myself.

Creating a safe space in my home has helped with that process. A place I can explore my soul and continue the healing process. Whether it's high vibrational frequency music on YouTube and meditation or doing some reflection and journalling – or even to read a book that shifts my soul – this space has become a place where I can just BE.

In one corner of my 'safe space' is my desk with business tools around me and lots of affirming words such as 'flourish', 'believe', and 'energise' pinned to the desk – along with pictures of my children at various stages of their lives. Against the back wall is my meditation area with lots of cushions, bookcases with my favourite books and mementos, and an abundance of incense sticks and essential oils.

I go through stages where I meditate daily and then at times only when I feel I need to. I've always been a spiritual person, but I felt I had to deny that part of me to survive. The universe has an amazing way of bringing it back to the forefront.

You know when you have a dream of what you want your life to be like? When I was younger I always felt powerless, but the feeling I was destined for more was there. Now I have the power to make that dream a reality, as I no longer must live someone else's dream or follow them to the ends of the earth and watch from the sidelines as my dreams fall by the wayside. No longer having to defend myself is an incredibly wonderful feeling.

I have the freedom to nurture close friendships with amazingly beautiful souls, whereas previously I felt I wasn't good enough. I'm learning to love who I am and no longer need to hide my true self. I'm learning to trust my instincts and not second-guess them. How freaking awesome is that?

One day, you find yourself just doing anything and everything to survive and then you seem to have this awakening and say, 'Wow! How did I achieve all this?'

I'm in awe of myself for achieving several qualifications in eight years. My incredible shining moment was when I was accepted into university. OMG! It was an enormous, validating moment. From being told I was 'better off getting a job' and being put down because I left high school at 14, to gaining enough knowledge and experience to be accepted into an undergrad program. That moment was like the song *Walking on Sunshine* by Katrina and the Waves. When you achieve a goal, the feeling you get is overwhelming empowerment. I was gobsmacked to achieve a credit in my first unit.

Later, I recognised that my true gifts were more aligned with inspiring and supporting others, and went on to create a business. Not only am I fulfilling my own life purpose, I'm healing my younger self at the same time, by being extremely brave and saying yes to opportunities that come my way.

I would like to take a moment though to say to you, gorgeous soul …

That's you, YES – YOU!

You are worth more than what has been said and done to you. You have so much to give, not only to yourself but also to others. You may not see it right now, and that's okay.

Nevertheless, there'll be a moment in your life, a quiet moment where you'll hear a little voice that says, 'I have a dream … I need to do this.' Believe in it, and create the most amazing life, one step at a time.

Don't stop believing. You've got this!

And finally, before I finish, there's one more sensational moment I would like to share with you. For one of my milestone birthdays I got to travel with a couple of girlfriends. I'd never been on a girls' trip away and to do it with amazing and inspiring women, OMG … WOW! Even though it rained every day we were there, I walked down to the beach every morning. I was in heaven!

One of my life goals was to go zip-lining through the rainforest. I had amazing luck when the rain cleared enough for me to achieve this enormous goal. A goal where I was able to conquer some major fears.

You may wonder, how did this make me feel? Nothing feels better than empowerment! Life's full of adventure now.

BELIEVE in yourself

There'll be a moment in your life, a quiet moment where you'll hear a little voice that says, 'I have a dream ... I need to do this.' Believe in it, and create the most amazing life, one step at a time.

Believe in yourself: You have been through so much. You can go through the recovery and healing to create your dream life.

Education: I achieved several qualifications. I learnt how to create a vision board. I listened to TED Talks and YouTube clips of people who had been working through their own life 'junk', people like Mel Robbins, Glennon Doyle and Brené Brown, just to name a few. I did all this even though I'd been told I was a poor student, and so can you.

Love yourself: This is not an easy thing to do, but loving yourself is more intoxicating than ending up in a toxic relationship. I fought like hell to uncover my truth, to see who I really am, to embrace the journey of self-discovery and to be happy being me. So can you.

Inspire: Inspire yourself daily by taking time to give yourself a safe space. In my safe space are lots of affirming words such as 'flourish', 'believe' and 'energise' pinned to the desk, along with pictures of my children at various stages of their lives. Each day, meditate or do some reflection and journaling – or even read a book that shifts your soul – give yourself space where you can just BE.

Empowerment: Nothing feels better than empowerment! When you achieve a goal, the feeling you get is overwhelming empowerment. Set small goals and build up to bigger goals – you will amaze yourself at what you can achieve.

Vibrational frequency music: Find and play vibrational frequency music from YouTube. This is believed to repair damaged tissues and cells within the body. The idea is that all matter is vibrating at specific frequencies, with depression and stress causing human beings to vibrate at a lower frequency. Playing higher frequency music is believed to promote healing. This type of music has helped me, and it may help you.

Embrace: Embrace help from a counsellor. I have had several counsellors throughout the years. Some got me to a place where I needed to be, and others were not such a good fit. There is a lot of inner work to do and you will be forever grateful for embracing this type of therapy in your life.

© Broken to Brilliant

CHAPTER EIGHT

MY POT OF GOLD AT THE END OF THE RAINBOW

'I am worthy of love and I have hope for the future.'

How does one live through the terror of domestic violence and abuse inflicted by a person you loved, trusted and vowed to spend the rest of your life with? How does one get through feeling anxious, frightened and completely broken, day after day for what seems like an eternity? How does one rebuild their life to find themselves again able to value every sunrise and every rainbow?

Over the last 20 years, I have lived two completely different lives. I was shattered and now I am shining.

My first life began when I met a charming, friendly guy at a barbecue. We had an instant connection. Being a single mum of a gorgeous baby, I wasn't looking for a relationship and was flattered by the attention. After chatting for hours, we exchanged phone numbers. It wasn't long before I, my baby and my new partner began going on family outings to the beach, the zoo and on picnics. I was feeling so happy and content with our little family unit. I thought, *This guy would not only be a great husband, he would be an amazing step-parent to my baby.*

We planned a future together which included building a house, getting married and having more children.

One day when we had been together for a year, I was in the kitchen cooking my homemade spaghetti bolognaise. The radio played in the background while my toddler and I danced around the kitchen together. My little one kept falling over in fits of laughter.

From nowhere my partner came charging towards me. He grabbed me around the throat, lifted me off my feet and slammed my head into the kitchen cupboard. My little one started screaming and crying as my partner dropped me to the floor and yelled, 'Turn that f__ing music down!'

He sat and ate dinner as if nothing had happened. He complimented me, and thanked me for cooking his favourite meal.

The next day he told me, 'That will never happen again,' and I believed him.

I kept myself busy and distracted by packing and preparing for the move into our new house. I was fully invested in our relationship and looking forward to a fresh start. I put all my energy into furnishing our forever family home. I had saved and budgeted so that we were able to purchase brand-new furniture such as a couch, TV, dining table and bedroom suite. The future looked bright.

On a gorgeous day, we got married in the presence of family and our closest friends. We had a reception full of laughter, great music, amazing food and champagne. It was a magical day – everything seemed perfect.

I fell pregnant soon after. During the very early stages of my pregnancy before announcing it to anyone, I had a tarot reading. The psychic said, 'Hi,' followed by, 'You're having a boy.' I thought to myself, *How do you know I'm pregnant?* I showed him a photo I had brought with me of my husband and me. After looking at it for not even 20 seconds he said, 'I don't know how to tell you this, but when I look at him I see "heil Hitler".' I knew exactly what he meant by those words.

We were blessed with our first child together; things seemed to be moving quickly, but it felt right and meant to be.

When my child was three months old, I woke after being slapped or punched in the face by my abuser. I questioned him the next morning, but he justified the abuse as 'not intentional'. He said, 'I was sleeping and didn't know what I was doing.'

What started as an occasional incident soon became a weekly, then a daily and nightly occurrence. I began to hear the words of the psychic in my head.

I put all my energy into dismissing, justifying and rationalising my abuser's behaviour. He put all his energy into controlling, dominating and dictating every aspect of our daily lives – what we did, when we did it and how we did it. He controlled our daily routine, our finances, our social life and our sexual relationship. I was told what to cook for dinner and where we were going on the weekend. Many times, he would say, 'Oh, by the way, I've invited mates over, so you need to go buy the food and grog. We need dinner – and snacks too. And clean up this f__ing house.'

It was exhausting raising young children, maintaining a functioning household and then having to clean, cook and cater for him and his mates. I would go to bed not long after I put the children to bed. I was unable to sleep, though, because after a few beers and bourbons my abuser, his mates and the music they played continuously got louder. I was too scared to say to them, 'Can you please keep the noise down?'

Over the next few months, my abuser demanded that I sit and socialise with him and his mates. He poured my drinks and, before I knew it, I would fall asleep on the couch and he would put me into bed. I would wake the following morning feeling extremely ill and hungover. On several occasions I woke in pain, bleeding from my bowel. My abuser would say to me, 'Last night was amazing.' I could never remember what had happened the night before.

I told him about the pain and bleeding: 'I think something is wrong and I need to go to the doctor.' He laughed; that was not the response I was expecting. He showed no concern, just complete coldness.

I began to dread night time when the sun went down. I woke in the middle of one night to feel him moving under the doona. I heard a clicking noise and felt his phone on my leg. I rolled over, knocking his phone to the floor, and said, 'What are you doing?'

He replied, 'Nothing, I just dropped my phone.'

My gut was screaming at me: *You need to check his phone.*

The footage I later found on his phone was horrifying and devastating; I ran to the bathroom and vomited. I was shattered. I felt violated and betrayed. I checked the video camera and computer where I found more sickening footage. I was so distraught I cried uncontrollably. In some of the footage I looked like I was dead; these images have haunted me for years. He secretly photographed and videoed himself sexually violating me while I was inebriated. I found out who and what caused my pain and bleeding from the bowel.

I could not tell him what I had discovered. I started making excuses so I wouldn't be forced to socialise with him and his mates. I took up night classes at the local gym and on occasion suffered a migraine headache. I did whatever I could to keep distance between us in the bed. I tried saying no to sexual intimacy. He would scream, 'You're a selfish b__h! What about my needs?' He would then throw the bed coverings onto the floor and walk out, slamming the door. I was left lying naked on the bed (I was not allowed to wear any nightwear). When I thought it was safe, I slowly crawled across to where my bedding was, picked it up and put it back on me. I lay there in fear waiting for him to come back into the bedroom, continue the verbal abuse and throw my bedding back on the floor, which is what happened on most occasions.

My children were in bed asleep at the other end of the house when this abuse occurred. If they were at a sleepover and it was only my abuser and me at home, the abuse was much more violent as he didn't need to hide it.

One night, my abuser arranged for the children to stay at a

friend's house so that we could go out for dinner. I was getting dressed when my abuser yelled at me, 'Why aren't you ready?'

I replied, 'I'm almost done.'

He charged at me, grabbed me by the arm while his other hand was around my throat, and threw me into the window. I thought I was going to die. My phone was within reach so I grabbed it and, for the first time in over ten years, I dialled 000. Sobbing and shaking uncontrollably, I asked for the police.

He walked out of the room, shouting, 'Call the f__ing police. I don't care.'

The police came and arrested him; I was left all alone at home. I was a complete mess with so many thoughts and emotions running through my head. *What happens now? What about the kids?*

The police put a family violence protection order on him, preventing him from coming to the marital home or coming in close contact with me.

I got the police to drop the order and allowed him back into the marital home and back into my heart – biggest regret of my life. I knew that this was far from a healthy, functioning relationship but I felt helpless and trapped. I honestly felt like I had a noose around my neck that he tightened and loosened when it suited him. I wasn't living but simply existing. I functioned like a robot he had programmed.

To family and friends, we had the perfect relationship. One of my closest friends who had been single for years actually said to me, 'I'm so jealous of you and your husband's relationship.' Like everybody else, she had no idea what was going on behind closed doors.

I smiled and laughed at family and social functions, but I was feeling miserable and broken on the inside. I was exhausted from putting on a facade. I hold strong values of truth and honesty in all my relationships, yet here I was doing the opposite.

I was a prisoner in his prison camp. My weight began to drop significantly, and my overall health was rapidly deteriorating.

My doctor arranged for me to have extensive health tests, including wearing a heart monitor. The results all came back inconclusive or normal. My mental health also deteriorated, and I began having severe anxiety and panic attacks. I had never previously experienced this and felt terrified and vulnerable.

I couldn't take it anymore – he had slowly chipped away at me for years taking away my self-worth, my confidence, my body and my mind. I was a dead person walking. It was time to get out and save myself, not only for me but for my children.

I put a plan in place to leave. In the final weeks of living in hell on earth, the abuse escalated. I endured being held down and sexually assaulted on more than one occasion, including while I was menstruating. I was not intoxicated during any of the assaults and can recall every ugly detail. I knew this was the beginning of the end and there was no going back from here.

I couldn't do this on my own, so I sought medical help. Finally, I confided in my general practitioner (GP) exactly what I was experiencing and how I was suffering; for him my medical conditions finally made sense. I completed a mental health care plan and was referred to counselling services and prescribed anti-anxiety medication. I was at my lowest point at this time. I had hit rock bottom. My GP asked me if I was suicidal. I responded,

'Absolutely not, but if I went to sleep and didn't wake up to experience this, then that's okay with me.'

What followed was years of constant court proceedings regarding the domestic violence and family law issues. My abuser used the court system as a further way of control and abuse. He contested every protection order I applied for and breached the conditions of each order. This resulted in him having to go to court after being charged with breaching the order on several occasions.

The consequence of his actions was that he had a criminal record, preventing future work and travel opportunities. He was furious and told family and friends, 'She is to blame for me not being able to get a management role,' and, 'This would never have happened if she didn't keep putting protection orders on me.' At no point did he accept responsibility. I honestly don't know what could have happened had I not had the protection of the court order.

He applied for custody of the children and I had no alternative but to fight for the safety of my children.

I found these constant legal battles emotionally, mentally and financially draining as well as completely soul-destroying. I didn't know if I was going to get through the process. At times I felt completely let down by the system. It felt like they were treating me as the person responsible for committing the domestic violence rather than the victim.

I couldn't see the light at the end of the tunnel. I remember feeling like I was in a deep, dark hole trying to claw my way to the top.

***

My second life began when I reached out to all the counselling and support services available locally. This included a psychologist, psychiatrist, women's domestic violence service, sexual assault victims' service and my GP. I followed all the advice I was given by the health professionals and used the coping strategies they recommended when I needed to. This included breathing and relaxation exercises as well as techniques such as tapping on my temples, cheeks, chin and collarbone when experiencing a panic attack or anxiety.

I felt that my counselling sessions were a safe place and that I finally had a voice that was heard.

No matter how traumatic or confronting it was to talk to my counsellor about the abuse, I knew this was essential in getting the best help, support and treatment for myself. It was crucial in my healing process.

I lived in regret for months after leaving, where I asked myself so many questions. Why did I allow it to happen? What could I have done so the abuse didn't happen? Why didn't I leave sooner than I did? I said to myself, 'I should have fought back. I should have left sooner.'

I allowed myself time to process those thoughts and then worked through them with my counsellor. Then I put them in the past where they belonged and started 'never living in regret'. Each day was a new day.

I clung to anybody I felt I could trust that offered me support. I took up offers of a shoulder to cry on and 'an open door' from family and friends.

I sought advice from the police about protecting my safety which led me to apply for a protection order, which I was granted and was able to extend for the following six years.

I identified triggers that would take me back to the domestic violence and abuse or would cause me to become anxious, fearful, nervous, unable to breathe or cause me to shake excessively. I lived for so long in constant fear and in fight-or-flight mode. I found myself screaming at him on the inside (fight) or I would disassociate as if I wasn't even present in that moment (flight). It took a couple of years of practising techniques and taking part in activities that helped me to relax and calm my mind to overcome the fight-or-flight mode. Meditation, walking, essential oils and crystals became my best friends.

I knew that I needed to let go and release all the toxicity. I did this by writing down how I was feeling. I also wrote letters to my abuser which I then destroyed – but felt much better getting the feelings and emotions out.

> 'Dear Abuser, it's me, the one you thought you had destroyed for good while you ran around town telling anyone and everyone how you were a loving and devoted husband and father and that you had to put up with my mental health issues. That's right, according to you – you were and are the victim. Well, guess what? I know who you really are. I've personally experienced your toxicity in all its abusive forms. I don't hate you or wish ill for you – you no longer exist to me. I will never allow you to take away or destroy my heart and soul again. I will recover. I will be the best form of

me without you. My conscience is clear. What about yours?'

I delved deep into myself to find the inner strength to go on. Sometimes, just to put one foot in front of the other was a huge challenge. I let go of the blame and shame and came to the realisation that I was not responsible for the abuse. He had to own that, not me. I never once asked to be abused or to be a victim of domestic violence – even though I was told by a close family member, 'What did you expect? You married him.'

I carefully looked at my relationships with family members and friends for those that were positive and supportive and those that weren't. I looked for any indication of a friendship or association with my abuser.

I became more aware of people's energies and stayed away from people who had toxic or negative energy. I focused on and nurtured the positive relationships in my life, as well as one with myself.

I learnt to love myself and be comfortable in my own skin. I took responsibility for how I was going to live my life. I was in control of my own destiny. Nobody else – just me.

I began making time for me and doing all the things I loved doing, like creative arts, reading novels, sitting on the beach listening to the ocean, going to see a movie, listening to my favourite music.

I took time to watch the sunrise, walk on the beach and in the water, and be thankful to the universe for all the beautiful things in my life that I was able to experience and enjoy.

I made positive dietary changes such as becoming a vegetarian to help give me the vitamins and nutrients I needed for a healthy body and mind.

My focus and energy on living a healthy, organic lifestyle meant I spent even less time on social media than I had previously. I changed the user names and passwords on my social media accounts.

While computers and technology weren't my forte and I had moved away from technology, I decided to go online and join a friendship group. That is where I met an amazing soul who I am fortunate to now call my partner.

I remember feeling so nervous. I was out of my comfort zone. I could barely use a computer and was a very private and shy person. My partner said that I 'glowed' when he first saw my photo. I had sent it to him in a private chat after chatting online and getting to know each other for a few weeks. When we first started dating, I disclosed very little about my past domestic violence relationship. I wanted him to know me for myself, not the domestic-violence me.

My past soon became evident as our relationship developed. I would wrap myself in a sheet every night to sleep, something I had done since leaving my abuser. I would wake up screaming after having a nightmare. I would shake or be unable to breathe for no apparent reason.

Though my abusive past managed to weave its way into my life, I found surrounding myself in love – a healthy and nurturing love – got me to where I am today. I AM WORTHY OF LOVE and I HAVE HOPE FOR THE FUTURE.

This is my journey: one who is so eternally grateful to the

universe for the beautiful people in my life and allowing me to experience the beauty of the rainbow.

Finding your pot of GOLD

My journey took me on many ups and downs, but I found my pot of GOLD at the end of the rainbow. The most valuable gold is that I have learnt I am worthy of love and I have hope for the future. You can share in this pot of gold at the end of the rainbow as you travel on your journey.

Get help: Contact all the counselling and support services available locally, such as a psychologist, psychiatrist, psychotherapist, counsellor, women's domestic violence service, sexual assault victims' service and your doctor. Follow their advice and use the coping strategies they recommend. For me, this included breathing and relaxation exercises as well as techniques such as tapping. When experiencing a panic attack or anxiety, I would tap on my temples, cheeks, chin and collarbone.

Organic lifestyle: Focus your energy on living a healthy, organic lifestyle. This includes spending less time on social media. Make positive dietary changes – becoming a vegetarian helped give me the vitamins and nutrients needed for a healthy body and mind. Make time for yourself. Do the things you love, such as creative arts, reading novels, sitting on the beach listening to the ocean, going to see a movie, listening to your favourite music, watching the sunrise, walking on the beach and in the water. Be thankful to the universe for all the beautiful things in life that you are able to experience and enjoy.

Love: Learn to love yourself and be comfortable in your own skin. Surround yourself with loving, healthy and nurturing relationships. This has got me where I am today. Love will wrap itself around you and carry you to your future.

Ditch regret and toxic relationships: Become more aware of people's energies and stay away from people who have a toxic or negative energy. Focus on and nurture the positive relationships in your life, as well as one with yourself. Never live in regret because this will prevent you from moving forward. I lived in regret for months after leaving, where I asked myself, 'Why did I allow it to happen?' and many more questions. Allow time to process those thoughts and then work through them with your counsellor. Put them in the past where they belong and start 'never living in regret'. Each day is a new day, with its own pot of gold.

© Broken to Brilliant

CHAPTER NINE

FINDING SPACE TO BE ME

'I am amazed I have not only survived, but am now thriving. I am most definitely a different person.'

'You threatened to kill your children.'

I looked at the psychiatrist as she spat out the words. I was in a room with about ten clinicians seated in a circle. They all looked down at their laps. No-one could look me in the face.

'No, I haven't,' I responded defiantly. 'That's ridiculous!'

'Well, this is what your file says.' She held up a manila folder and thumped it down on a desk. 'I'm putting you under a compulsory treatment order and you are not permitted to leave the ward because you are a flight risk.'

I knew where the accusation had come from. My husband had found out I'd been talking to domestic violence counsellors and was planning to leave. He told the psychiatrists that my allegations of domestic violence were paranoid delusions and signs of mental illness. According to the doctors, he was concerned, worried, and loved and cared for me deeply. This kind man would never hurt me. 'He is your carer,' they told me.

Boy, he was convincing. And this wasn't the first time. The

mental hospital was on speed dial on his mobile. Anytime I stepped out of line, he was on the phone to them. Then psychiatric nurses and police would be on my doorstep to haul me away to the nuthouse. All this in front of my crying children, while he consoled them that Mummy was very sick in the head, but not to worry as we would visit her in the mental hospital.

He did his research. He decided I had bipolar disorder, googled the symptoms and regurgitated them to the doctors using the medical terms they loved. According to him, my normal, happy, outgoing personality was the manic phase. My saving up for weeks for a watch and buying it against his wishes was a 'manic spending spree'. My crying after his abuse was obviously the depressive phase of the illness.

He also threw in generous helpings of outrageous beauties like these: I was psychotic; I neglected and abused the children; I had a knife and had threatened to stab him and the kids; I lay around all day and did nothing; I was violent and abusive to him; and the best one – he was the victim.

The psychiatrists bought it and I was locked up – 'for the sake of the children', they said.

On one occasion, I was locked up for two months away from my children. It was one of the most traumatising experiences of my life, like being a criminal in a maximum-security prison. There was a concreted verandah where you could go outside for fresh air, but even that was surrounded by bars and barbed wire.

I was put in a ward with violent men who paced back and forth yelling that they were going to kill somebody. I thought that 'somebody' would be me. Sometimes they smashed stuff. I had to share showers and toilets with them – with no locks on the doors.

The staff forced me to take strong medication. They also forced me to get blood tests every day to prove I was taking the medication.

The nurses searched me and my possessions regularly for drugs and weapons. Creepy guys followed me around asking for my phone number and whether we could hook up after we got out. The communal kitchen crawled with cockroaches.

If any of us complained about our treatment, we were threatened with being locked up in isolation. The more I told the doctors about his abuse, the longer they kept me in there. I learnt to shut my mouth and go along with it until finally they let me out.

***

I only realised it was domestic violence from talking to counsellors from 1800 RESPECT. I would ring them after every incident of abuse and when I felt myself falling into despair. As I would sob, telling them what he was doing to me, they would say over and over, kindly, 'Darling, that's domestic violence and you don't deserve that.'

What really hit home for me was seeing two diagrams one of the counsellors emailed to me: the Duluth Power and Control Wheel and Walker's Cycle of Violence. There it was in black and white – all of his behaviours that made me feel like I was a character in an M. Night Shyamalan movie.

There was a lot more to it than just physical violence. There was minimising and denying the abuse; blaming me for everything; telling me the abuse never happened; putting me down; telling me I was mentally ill; isolating me from my friends and support networks; threats to take the children from me; hurting the children; acting like the king; smashing things; intimidation; making me fearful; giving me an allowance and making me account for every cent I spent even though he burnt through money.

I was shocked there were actual names for the things he was doing to me and that these were behaviours common to abusers – a prescribed set of tactics. I was in a state of denial for a long time. I couldn't accept that the man I loved would actually do these things deliberately to hurt me. If only I could be a better wife, a better mother, a better person in every way, I could fix this relationship.

It took me nearly 20 years to leave that relationship. I lost track of the number of times I left and returned. Every time I went back, it got worse. The violence and abuse got more frequent and the lengths he would go in order to control me became more extreme.

Once, I went into a refuge but it only lasted two weeks. He knew how to work the system and he used the same three tactics every time – money, children and the legal system. He cancelled my credit card, closed our joint bank accounts and put all the money into an account in his name. He hired a lawyer and got a court order by lying to the judge that the kids were in danger from me – the same old stuff that I was crazy, violent and an unfit mother. Six police officers, brandishing the order, stormed the refuge, bringing him with them. They took the children from me and handed them over to him. They also took my car off me.

My kids were aged one, three and five. Two were still in

nappies or pull-ups. I had just finished weaning my youngest. He had no idea how to care for them. He had barely lifted a finger at home. The judge gave him full custody and only allowed me to see the kids for about three hours a week, on the proviso I was supervised by my mother. The judge based that decision on his testimony.

Sure enough, a week or so later he phoned, telling me I was a selfish, lazy b___ and demanding I come home and look after the kids. How was he supposed to work full-time, take care of the house and look after the kids? 'You only think of yourself,' he said. So I went back.

But I didn't go back for him – I went back for my kids.

***

I got a life-threatening reaction to the bipolar medication I had been forced to take for a mental illness I didn't have. It left me permanently disfigured, disabled and with a range of incurable diseases. I previously had perfect health – a vegetarian who never smoked, rarely drank alcohol and loved running and lifting weights.

The sicker I got, the more violent and malevolent he became towards me. The bright side was, I was now off those f__ing meds, and no doctor could ever force me to take them again. All of my doctors now say I never even had bipolar in the first place.

A light-bulb moment came when my counsellor did a domestic violence risk assessment which involved a series of questions. I scored extremely high. She told me he was one of the most dangerous men she had come across in terms of control. She said I was in real danger of being killed and suggested I never be alone with him.

When I got my cancer diagnosis I cried, and he embraced me and said he would be there for me. That lasted about a day. Then the fury and hatred came out. The next night he was beside himself with rage that I hadn't carried his dinner over to him as he sat at the dining table, waiting.

I said, 'You're acting as though you're a victim.'

He said, 'I am the victim.'

At first, I thought the cancer was going to be terminal and I didn't have much time left. The two things that frightened me the most were the prospect of dying before I had the chance to do all the things I wanted to do in my life, and not being there to protect and care for my kids. I hadn't yet left the abusive relationship because I'd been hanging in there until my youngest turned 18.

About a week after my cancer diagnosis, he violently assaulted me. He roared at me that I was a dumb b___ and kicked a hole in our bedroom door while I was trying to hide from him. My sin? I had turned the fan off.

I called the police and they came. He told them this big story about how he was the victim and I had terrorised and violently assaulted him. The police gave me a lecture telling me I needed to sort it out with him, and then they left. The next morning, my children said their poor dad explained that I had attacked him and made that hole in the door and that I had anger issues. When I told them it wasn't true, they called me a liar.

He booked a beach holiday with the kids to coincide with

my cancer treatment. I begged him not to go as I needed his support, but he went anyway. I had to beg friends for lifts to and from the hospital. I had to wait alone for major medical tests. When the doctor told me the cancer hadn't spread, I burst into tears of relief. While I was in hospital, my husband texted me a photo of our child pretending to be dead. When I saw it, I felt like vomiting.

I later discovered that while I was in hospital, he had a lady friend visit to cook, clean, take care of the children and have sex with him.

He punched our youngest child in the mouth, breaking a tooth, and said if I reported him, he would get a protection order against me and file for full custody of the children. I did report it to the police. They did nothing, and he did exactly what he said he would.

All that time, I stayed for my kids. I knew if I left he would take them from me and I would not be able to keep them safe.

But I had to accept that if I stayed, I could end up dead. I knew this man would eventually kill me.

He was really excited about my trauma insurance money which was due to come in soon. He said he would quit his job, take our kids out of school and travel around Australia. Imagine how much happier he would be with the massive payout he'd get if I was dead.

Because of my illness, I had to give myself regular injections. I was terrified he would inject me with an overdose in my sleep, which would kill me. It would be the perfect murder because he could blame my illness. If I died, there would be an outpouring of sympathy for him and he would once again be the victim – a role he relished. I slept in my kids' rooms with a mobile phone under my pillow. I lived in a constant state of terror and high alert – ready to fight or flee.

***

As crazy as it sounds, getting cancer and then being served with a farcical application for a domestic violence order ended up being a blessing because it gave me a chance to escape.

The day the trauma insurance money hit our bank account, I transferred it to an account in my name. I used this money to live on for the next two years and to pay for legal representation.

Two weeks after I finished my cancer surgery and treatment, I was at home making lunch for the kids while my husband lay in bed reading. I was weak from my treatment, had lost all my hair and weighed about 40 kilograms. A police officer knocked on the door. He handed me a legal document requiring my response – my husband's application for a domestic violence order, filled with pages of lies about how violent I was towards him and the children, and how my husband was frightened and wanted me out of the house. The magistrate had denied him an emergency order, thank God, setting a court date to hear his application instead.

Straight away, I asked the officer whether I and the kids could leave. He said there was nothing to stop us. I quickly loaded the kids and a few meagre possessions into my humble hatchback. With the officer present, there was nothing my husband could do to me, and I could tell he was panicking. He hadn't expected this.

The officer asked whether my husband could say goodbye to the kids. 'Sure, he can say goodbye,' I said. My husband created a massive scene, crying and carrying on, upsetting the children.

So that was that. I was gone, finally, after over 20 years with that a__hole. This time I knew I would never go back to him. No matter what.

I will never forget the day I was granted my order against him. His farcical application was eventually thrown out by the magistrate. Instead, Her Honour found that I had been subjected to 20 years of physical, verbal, emotional, sexual and financial abuse and she granted me a domestic violence order with full conditions. My lawyer said she had never seen that before. Her Honour said that his application against me was an act of domestic violence and warned that, if it continued, jail would be the consequence. It was awesome.

***

Looking back, throughout most of that marriage I blamed myself for everything.

Whenever I tried to leave, I would get dragged back by him and the systems that were supposed to support me, but actually facilitated his abuse. I believed the only way I would be able to escape him was if I committed suicide.

But at the same time, he was like a drug. When I met him, I thought he was gorgeous, and I fell hard. He was charming and funny, and he chased me relentlessly.

From the outside, we looked like the perfect family. We lived in a beautiful home and travelled the world. We had three beautiful children. He held a respected position in the church and would often give the sermons.

So when he would swear at me, call me a dumb b___, tell me to shut my mouth, to go f___ myself, and that I was pathetic, lazy and selfish, then not talk to me for days; when he would hit me with the door, knee me in the stomach, pick me up and hurl me against the wall, pull me out of the car and throw me to the ground and nearly run me over; when he would punch and kick holes in the walls – it felt like a nightmare.

When I went to the elders in our congregation, they didn't believe me. It was a patriarchal religion which taught that the man was the head of the house and the wife had to be submissive. According to them the wife's role was to cook, clean, satisfy the husband sexually and have babies and raise them. An education and a career for a woman was a definite no-no. She was to know her place and be happy to be in that place. Being in that religion kept me trapped in that marriage for longer than I should have been.

***

There were lots of signs of domestic violence I dismissed or made excuses for.

It started with the hot and cold treatment. One minute attentive and loving, the next, sullen and aggressive. And of course, it was always my fault.

Then the heavy drinking. When I expressed my worries, he would dismiss my concerns and drink even more, telling me I was the reason he drank.

If he conned someone and got away with it, he would brag about it.

There was the gaslighting. When I confronted him – about swearing at me, for example – he would tell me it never happened. 'I'm really worried about you,' he would say. 'I really think you should see someone about your mental problems.' At first I thought I was not remembering correctly, but I started keeping a diary so I could prove to myself that I was not going nuts.

I overlooked his controlling behaviour, because I thought it was showing he cared for me. He wouldn't let me have a mobile phone for a long time. When I eventually got one, I wasn't allowed to make any calls from it. My phone was only for him to contact me.

He put me down in front of friends and family. When I said it hurt my feelings, he would say, 'Lighten up! You can't even take a joke!'

There was the typical love bombing at the start. He said he loved me after two weeks and was talking about marriage after three months. At the time I thought, 'Well, this guy knows what he wants.' He coerced me into physical intimacy much faster than I would have liked.

Oh yes, and the old classic – his ex-girlfriend was a 'nut job'. Now I know that all abusers say that about their previous victims. He says it about me now.

I had doubts the whole time we were going out, but I squashed them down. I ignored my gut instinct, and I deeply regret that.

***

My supports and help:
- My mum let me and my kids live with her for over two years after I left the abusive relationship.
- My dear friends, most of whom were other mums from my kids' school, stood by me. One lovely friend let me stay with her for two months.
- My wonderful family doctor (GP), psychologist and psychiatrist believed me, advocated for me and stuck up for me against the claims I was mentally ill. They all wrote affidavits detailing his abuse and testifying that I don't have bipolar disorder.
- Wonderfully kind, patient counsellors from domestic violence support lines listened to me, validated me and taught me that the way he treated me was actually domestic violence. They stuck by me despite the many times I left and went back to my abuser and vacillated between defending and protecting him and hating him.
- A handful of Domestic Violence Liaison Officers from the police encouraged me to follow through with my domestic violence application, as did court support staff.
- The women's shelter that took my children and me in.
- I visited websites and video blogs about narcissistic abuse, such as Echo Recovery, the Little Shaman, Shahida Arabi from Self Care Haven, Sam Vacnic (a self-confessed narcissist who explains narcissistic tactics and how to deal with them), Richard Grannon from Spartan Life Coach and Meredith Miller from Inner Integration. All of these people taught me that abusers have very clear methods of

operating. I learnt how to put myself first for a change, how to set and maintain boundaries and how to detach from post-separation abuse. I learnt about gaslighting, trauma bonding, flying monkeys, triangulation, projection, word salad and many other terms in the world of narcissistic abuse.

- Books such as *Why Does He Do That?* by Lundy Bancroft and *Taming Toxic People* by David Gillespie helped me accept there was nothing I could have done to stop the abuse – that the responsibility lay with him. The book *Broken to Brilliant* which I borrowed from the council library opened my eyes to the fact that other women have gone through the same thing and survived.
- The organisation RizeUp gave me furniture and white goods when I eventually moved into my own rental.
- A dear lady who worked at the Department of Housing took responsibility for my case and arranged for me to get a bond loan and a grant of several weeks' rent.

I am amazed I have been through what I have and not only survived, but am now thriving. I am most definitely a different person than I was when I was in that relationship. I have surprised myself by my courage and bravery, my strength, my strong sense of justice and fairness, and that I am willing to speak out about things that are wrong. I am extremely strong and resilient. I now get validation from myself and don't need it from others as much. I was funny before the abuse and that is now coming back. I love making people laugh. I am badass, smart, capable, sure of myself, fiercely loyal, a mama bear, fearless, strong. I stand up for myself and those I love. I don't believe in religion or an afterlife anymore and that is very freeing for me because it makes me value my life and my time on this earth as precious and finite. I was able to get away and have another go at life – this time, a life I want.

Some of the key things I did that helped me move forward:
- I got regular counselling from qualified domestic violence counsellors.
- I set goals and created action plans to reach those goals.
- I started doing nice things for myself, such as getting my nails done or buying myself flowers.
- I got a new set of friends who do not know my abuser and who believe, validate, and support me.
- I reconnected with trusted old friends I had abandoned during the hard times.
- I cut ties with anyone who was friends with my abuser – which included unfriending them on Facebook.
- I said yes to all invitations from friends to go out to festivals, concerts and events.
- I started working out at the gym.
- I got a full-time job.
- I changed back to my maiden name.
- I applied and was accepted into a further degree, and undertook other studies that will allow me to help other women leaving domestic violence.
- I bought my first car on my own – one that I chose in a model and colour I like – with my own money and registered in my name only. Every time I look at it and

drive it, I feel happy. This is so weird because I am not normally a materialistic person and I don't like to attach myself to possessions.

- I started reading books again – books I like and I choose.
- I started playing the piano again. I play songs I like and I choose.
- I buy what I like – and I answer to nobody about my purchases.
- I started playing loud upbeat music at home and singing and dancing around at home like I used to.

My next major goal is to buy my own house.

***

My life is completely different without the abuse. I never thought it would be like this. I feel genuinely joyful. If the electricity bill needs paying, it is up to me to pay it. If a light bulb needs changing, I change it. The money in my bank account is there because of me. I earned it and I am responsible for how it is spent. I don't have to stress about not having money because it has gone on alcohol or fishing trips.

I love having my own peace and quiet at home. My place is modest and all my furniture was donated by a charity, but it is MY place. I can decorate it the way I want. I buy myself flowers and put them in a vase and every time I see them it makes me happy.

I love sitting in my bedroom, reading and looking out the window, and listening to rain or to music. It is so peaceful and it is MY SPACE.

I threw a massive house-warming party and I invited everyone I liked and whoever had supported me. It was so much fun.

One night, I took my children to the markets. I loved the twinkling lights and the roving street performers. We watched a magician, and then members of the audience were invited onstage to compete in a dance battle. So I got up on stage and did it! And I was awesome! I felt like I was representing all the mums out there. When I went back to my seat, other mums high-fived me and said, 'You were the best!'

I could be silly and ridiculous and funny and that was alright. It was such a great night with my kids and I knew this was what I had wanted, and I had got it. I was finally happy again, my kids were happy, and I knew it would be okay.

Being me in MY SPACE

I was able to get away and have another go at life – this time a life I wanted. I was able to focus on things for me and the children. I was able to be me, in MY SPACE. Having my own space helped me get back to being me. I am amazed that I have not only survived but am now thriving. I am most definitely a different person than I was when I was in that relationship. I have surprised myself at my courage and bravery, my strength. You will surprise yourself too when you break free to be you, and allow laughter back into your life.

Memories: Do activities that are good for you and your children. This will help you to create new, happy and positive memories for both yourself and your children. Create a memorable home environment; make it your space. It should feel peaceful, safe, quiet and homey. Decorate it the way you want and let the children decorate their rooms the way they want.

Yourself: Care for yourself and let the inner you out. Buy some nice things for yourself, get your nails done, buy yourself some flowers, take time out for yourself. Make yourself a new set of friends who do not know your abuser and who believe, validate, and support you.

Support: Seek out support from services and have regular counselling from qualified domestic violence counsellors. Get help to set up and furnish your home. Contact the domestic violence support services in the back of this book to guide you.

Plan and participate: Create action plans to achieve your goals. Get up and participate in your life. Dance and laugh, play the piano. Choose your own cool, fun things to do.

Accept: Accept that you are not responsible for their behaviour, you cannot change them, there was nothing you could have done to stop the abuse, the lies, the deceit. Accept that the responsibility for their behaviour lies with them.

Connect: Throw a party, connect with neighbours and friends, go to the markets or somewhere you all love – it does not have to cost money. Maybe walk in the park, play on the play equipment, build sandcastles on the beach with your kids.

Education: Educate yourself on domestic violence and narcissism. Use the many websites available, such as Echo Recovery, the Little Shaman, Shahida Arabi from Self Care Haven, Sam Vacnic (a self-confessed narcissist who explains narcissistic tactics and how to deal with them), Meredith Miller from Inner Integration. Also, books such as *Why Does He Do That?* by Lundy Bancroft and *Taming Toxic People* by David Gillespie helped me understand the situation I was in. The book *Broken to Brilliant* which I borrowed from the council library opened my eyes to the fact that other women have gone through what I have gone through and survived. Go back and study to support your future directions.

CHAPTER TEN

HOME AT LAST

'I acknowledge and accept. Yet I will never forget. I am thankful. I embrace radical self-acceptance, learning the skills to reframe my shame of self-aversion and discovering true refuge.'

I AM IN A SWIRLING UNFOCUSED STATE, DISORIENTATED, DRIFTing in and out of consciousness. Surrounded by people. Music playing.

I look up and see him, leaning back against the bar, arms extended. I will never forget the look on his face. Depraved satisfaction.

[Blackout]

I am vomiting, slumped forward in a kneeling position as a man pulls my hair.

There are two other men.

He is fully clothed, leaning back against the bedroom wall. He announces, 'The party is over, boys.'

[Blackout]

I am being gently carried.

He says, 'I'm so proud of you.'

***

When I told my sister this story years later, she held my hand. She looked at me and said, 'He drugged you and had you gang-raped.' I cried.

After a year of what I thought was a passionate and respectful relationship, this was my first experience of sexual violence. It signalled the pathway that lay ahead.

'It's time to step out,' became his commanding code.

At a bar he spotted his mark and said, 'Him.' It was my job to recruit, and most times I pulled it off.

One night I was unsuccessful. Drunk, having been plied with alcohol, I was told to sit in the back of the car. He drove around the city, stopping when he saw potential, 'I have a woman in the back. Why don't you hop in?'

Lying down pretending to be asleep. My mind in a loop: *Please don't get in.*

'Nope, she looks doped and asleep. Forget that s___,' one of the men answered.

***

My life was not always full of violence – I was cared for with empathy in my previous marriage. We worked hard. Saved for a deposit, moved into our own home and realised a dream. I was loved and felt blessed. We shared mutual passions and revelled in time spent alone, balanced by celebrations of significant events with family. We experienced the contentment of valued friends.

My husband showed great empathy when I experienced periods of clinical depression. He understood my need for quietude to manage my struggles. Once, I spent a full winter's day in the bath reading the latest book awarded the Man Booker Prize. He came in with a steaming pot to add to the chilled water.

'I'm disappearing again,' I said, my voice reflecting my inevitable descent.

'Remember what it's like to come back,' he reassured. 'You need to write.' He knew the form of renewal I required.

As our marriage advanced we realised we were infertile. We were denied the role of parents in the 'circle of life'. Our relationship became tinged with melancholy.

***

My abuser and I met at work. He was a casual employee. One year later, I offered him a full-time position on a collaborative project. As I progressed through my career we would become 'more than colleagues'.

I was intrigued by this man of separated worlds – work life, fatherhood, uncomfortable in society.

As we worked together, I felt myself drawn to him. I was overwhelmed by a relentless and intense infatuation.

I did not break my marriage vows but spoke to my husband.

'Is it the man at your work?' he queried.

'Yes. But I've spoken to him and he's not interested,' I replied.

'We both know our marriage is over. I'm sorry he doesn't want a relationship. I just want you to be happy.' Even at this time my husband was gracious and kind.

I continued to pursue the man who would become my abuser. One evening he said, 'My life is chaos. You don't want to get involved with me.' He warned me, yet I did not heed his advice.

When I met his father he said, 'Please don't tell me you are in a relationship with my son?'

'Yes,' I said.

'Let me tell you one thing,' he cautioned. '"What a tangled web he weaves."'

I didn't know what he meant and was confused by his attitude.

I fell in love with this man. I was naive. I did not foresee the danger that lay ahead. His three separated worlds became four, and I was one of them.

I did not understand I was experiencing domestic violence. I continued to make allowances for his behaviour. I thought his actions might be normal for a creative person. When he insisted we keep our relationship a secret from our work colleagues, it made me feel treasured, covert. I was his and his alone.

After six months I was given permission to tell my family about my relationship, but it remained hidden from our work colleagues.

I became pregnant. Finally, a longed-for child. This gift was not by chance – he had supported me fully in trying to have a baby. When I started to 'show' I asked what I should say at work.

'Tell them you used a sperm donor,' he said with distress.

'No. What will people think when our child comes in and calls you Dad?' I replied. I revealed our relationship to my workmates. It was the first time I had disobeyed him.

I had complications during my pregnancy but continued to work until the morning before I went into hospital. Following discharge after the birth of our baby, I returned that same evening to intensive care due to complications. He stayed the first night but slept in the patients' lounge.

When I had improved enough to return to the maternity ward, our employer phoned, and was shocked that my partner was not by my side. He gave my partner time off work, and insisted that he provide me with support. My partner visited for a short time each day and sat in a chair with his back to me. He did not speak. I cried and continued to ask him why this was so. He ignored me. I rationalised that he had always been phobic with all things medical.

Seven weeks after the birth, the father of our child announced, 'I never wanted this child. I can't afford the mortgage. Go back to work.'

***

I began to fear that the sexual violence would resume, and our home environment now included a troubled stepchild. My partner's child from another marriage had run away from home due to fear of my partner's ex-wife. The child was found weeks later, asleep on a beach in another state, and would only agree to return if they could live with me and my partner.

I tried to establish a stable home, but despite my best efforts, our home life continued to deteriorate. My partner seemed oblivious to the depth of my stepchild's trauma, and behaviours that began to threaten my baby's physical safety.

I had to remove my child from danger. I visited my mother and discussed the problems. My mother accepted my baby into her loving arms and raised him full-time from seven weeks until three years of age.

I protected myself by burying myself in my work. I worked six days per week, averaging 70 hours at work and bringing more work home. I existed on three hours' sleep per night.

I would collect my child from my parents' home on Saturday evenings, and we would spend Sundays together. During my annual leave I would escape with our child on holidays. As our baby grew into a toddler, my partner became a more interested parent. I found this a baffling duality of his personality.

***

I spoke to my new boss. I felt the weight of depression, unable to endure the relentless pressure and extended hours worked during the last ten years.

My boss was surprised that I had depression and refused to give me leave. He refused access to my long service leave. It was a humiliating year as I battled to claim workers compensation or superannuation, but to no avail.

Yet within this crisis an unexpected gift arose.

I joined Weight Watchers. I overcame fear. Anxiously, I attended meetings with an inspirational leader and she gave me hope. I was open about my depression and experienced supportive company. I achieved my exercise goals, tracked my food intake and learnt how to cook again – an activity I once enjoyed. I became fit. My depression improved.

And …

Our child came home. The delight of a four-year-old, finally returned to me.

On weekends a riot of neighbourhood children invaded. Our

child – the youngest – plus six others ranging from four to 15 years, and our dog adored by the children.

I made friends with my neighbours and began to attend the local church. We were part of a community.

I no longer slept with my partner. I moved into my child's bedroom and we shared a bunk bed with a jungle of toys hanging from the slats above. We had long conversations. I read to my child. I was safe at night.

I re-read a book purchased during my first marriage, Thomas Moore's *Care of the Soul: A Guide for Cultivating Depth and Sacredness in Everyday Life*.[32] I annotate my books, and date the notes, so I was able to compare my life then and now.

In the 1990s, I saw that I had learnt to recognise and implement a new approach to thinking about everyday activities. I was able to appreciate their therapeutic nature. I discovered great meaning and established a sense of the sacred in what I previously perceived as mundane and perfunctory tasks. It was a strategy that greatly reduced my intermittent periods of clinical depression.

In the 2000s, I saw that my profound knowledge implemented during my previous marriage had vanished and been replaced by crippling demons. I had to push myself to perform household chores. I wore cement boots.

I gathered my family together. 'I'm leaving him and selling the house,' I stated numbly. With deep shame, I shared my life of sexual violence.

My mother, herself a victim of childhood domestic violence,

understood. She knew she had protected my child and in doing so, had saved my life.

After ten years I finally left. I sold my home and ran towards freedom. I imagined a life shared with my child, no longer just snatched moments.

***

I crashed, and found a psychiatrist who admitted me to hospital with clinical depression. He concentrated on exploring the best antidepressant to improve my condition.

Because I had been admitted to hospital, I had to return my child to live with my ex-partner. As an inpatient during an eight-week stay, I met my psychologist and revealed the full extent and duration of the abuse. As I sobbed she said to me, 'He stripped you of your humanity.'

The hospital I attended was a unique multidisciplinary mental health facility that was calming, caring and therapeutic, with a focus on recovery. I finally received an accurate diagnosis of bipolar disorder and post traumatic stress disorder (PTSD).

Following my diagnosis, I read Blake Levine's book *Beating Bipolar: How One Therapist Tackled his Illness … and How What he Learned Could Help You*.[33] After reading the first words in his introduction, I ticked all the boxes – the 'hyper-frenzied highs, paralysing lows, and periods of normalcy'. The uncharacteristic behaviour that could occur. Unbridled energy and sleeplessness, cycling into depression that erodes self-confidence and weighs you down.

I read Beyond Blue's definition of PTSD as a particular set of reactions that can develop in people who have been through a traumatic event which threatened their life or safety, or that of others around them. As a result, the person experiences feelings of intense fear, helplessness or horror.[34]

***

I have had to return to live with him twice since I left him, because of my mental illness and homelessness.

But that also meant I could return to my child. At night we shared a futon and I held on tight. Crying after my child went to sleep, I would say in my head, 'Let me be worthy.'

The sexual abuse? No longer, because my child was now old enough to bear witness.

When a community mental health nurse joined my mental health team, the scope of my experiences finally became apparent and I began to comprehend my life with my ex-partner.

He was a predatory sociopath and had inflicted upon me not only sexual violence, but psychological, emotional, social and financial abuse. The nurse explained that sociopaths know how to pick their victims.

I was hoodwinked. He established the tone. Set the line. Attached the lure. I took the bait. He reeled me in.

I continue to see my psychologist. She helps me reframe my successive admissions to hospital not as failures but as progress.

With acceptance, I now recognise my admissions as a call to rest. To surrender to the depths of the drift and look for the elusive gaps between the sounds.

I have provided you with the profile of a monster. My story is true. If I were to discuss this with him he would deny it. Yet we would both know this world he lives in, then retreats from, is real.

As I reflect on my experience of domestic violence, having left then returned twice, at times I am consumed by anger and grief.

I was subjected to relentless sexual assault. I had become a 'sex slave' in suburbia. He dispensed continued verbal, psychological, emotional, social and financial violence. I was belittled, degraded, and demoralised. I was held captive and tortured.

I lost my home. I was denied the right to raise my child. I lost my mind and attempted suicide three times and, homeless, I had to return twice. I lost myself.

***

I was approved for a disability pension, which enabled me to afford private health insurance and return to a private hospital.

I battled through three years to find a medication regime that provided me with relative stability. I have had more than ten admissions, including two in public hospitals when I was homeless.

What has been pivotal to my recovery is the re-established contact with my mental health care team (psychiatrist, psychologist and community mental health nurse).

I see my psychiatrist frequently when my mood, rapid cycling, PTSD symptoms and medication interactions are reviewed. We share engaging conversation over coffee at his practice.

I implemented strategies recommended by my psychologist. She listens to my story and sets gentle tasks with a report back at our next appointment. Her treatment is a seamless implementation of several types of behaviour therapy, mindfulness and meditation, grief counselling and radical acceptance.

I established a meditation retreat. A raised garden bed, shaded by a rambling orange trumpet vine. I planted seeds. I tended to their needs. I watched them grow. They nourished my soul.

I walked, taking 'mindfulness' photos. Capturing moments representing emerging confidence or anguish. I had them printed and created small photo books.

The role of my community mental health nurse is crucial. He is my case coordinator, liaising with my psychiatrist and psychologist. A community setting provides a different environment from a clinical setting. It is the world I live in. He helps to reinforce my need to establish a home haven. We identify my triggers and coping strategies. He helps me establish goals and listens as I read my writing. He helps me believe that I may one day become a published author. In addition to face-to-face contact we regularly text and email.

I renewed two friendships and glimpsed hope.

A weekly text from my friend: 'Coffee? No pressure. Are you writing?' I met her when our children started school. When I became unwell, she remained my friend when others walked away.

I re-established a friendship with another friend. A victim of the silent epidemic of domestic violence against men, with lived experience of mental illness. He helped me find trust and feel safe. We have fun on rambling day trips and have shared a holiday together.

My child said, 'Mum, it's time for you to leave.' He had seen the frightening deterioration in my health and knew more than I had recognised. If I did not escape, I would sink into the abyss forever, never to return to him.

At times it seems that my only achievement has been to survive. But with the help of my community mental health nurse and after further contemplation, I recognise success and triumph.

Over coffee recently with a past work colleague and my closest friend at that time, I disclosed my reality of domestic violence. She was astonished to hear 'behind the scenes'. She said, 'You were such an inspiration to me. Compassionate and understanding, and funny. Someone never to be forgotten who changed my life. You treated each of us as a person.'

I am strong and resilient.

When I returned to live with him for the second time, I was severely unwell. Around this time my child completed an assignment on mental health. The topic – bipolar. Following the assignment he came to me and said he had bipolar and wanted to see a psychiatrist. My partner disagreed. I found the strength, stepped up and became an advocate for my child.

I fought for my son and won.

***

I acknowledge and accept. Yet I will never forget.

I am thankful.

My mother has now died, but I know she would be proud of my achievements. Others consider them as a life of failed potential. She would be proud of my child and understand that although my child now lives with their father (through mutual agreement between me and my child), we are in our own way a family.

My child's father provides the stable home required by a child with bipolar disorder. He pays for school, sport, health and recreation. Despite a difficult childhood, my child has a list of sporting and academic achievements. I was excited to be shown an important award as my child said, 'Look at this. It's not just a piece of paper but a medallion too. And it's engraved!'

My life changed when I moved into an affordable housing apartment, a safe, secure space. My own.

I used my superannuation to establish myself. I had the power to transform the aesthetic compatibility of my home. White walls of a quiet mind. A slow and steady revolution to inner peace.

My new home fostered an improvement in my physical and mental health. My brain 'awoke'.

I established enduring friendships.

I began to write again as part of my return to wellness. A daily reflection in a simple dialogue-based form of creative writing. My sophistication evolving or simplifying as best applied.

I created a small online group to publish my work.

I was able to rethink my direction. My mind cognisant that driven flights into wellness may not be my own. With insight I had to be hypervigilant and recognise that my experience of 'happiness' may represent a mood elevation with the potential for mania.

Instead, I focus on slow and steady progress – no hurry – with time to meander.

I have since moved again into a new unit. It provides a more well-suited community with measured company and provides the opportunity for the extended solitude I require. Solitude reduces overstimulation and helps me remain as stable as possible.

Nestled within a planned environment of walking paths surrounded by trees. 'Good morning' greetings along the busy trails are part of my morning ritual.

My child recently said to me, 'This new place is perfect for you. I know something very bad happened to you … but please … don't ever tell me.'

My suffering acknowledged, I embraced Tara Brach's approach[35] to radical self-acceptance: mindfulness, self-love and self-forgiveness; learning the skills to reframe my shame of self-aversion and discovering true refuge.

***

Six months before my child's 16th birthday, I asked what they wanted as a gift. An idea was forming but I would need to budget to ensure its realisation.

'To go to the holiday park just for the day,' my child said with a grin. 'When I was living with Nan you would take me there on our holidays every day. I just want to see the animals again.'

Bingo! I was right. We would go to the holiday park, but not for a day. I purchased two annual passes.

We celebrated his birthday with the family.

Gift time.

'Check your email and you'll see my gift.' I was eager to see his reaction.

'Oh my God!' my child said.

'I figured one day at holiday park wasn't enough. We'll plan a holiday in January.'

My ex-partner looked at me. It was clear that he was angry with me. Body tense and eyes downcast, he seemed dismayed that I had made a decision not contingent upon his existence. My child would experience choice. We would share time together away from the 'set schedule' environment of living with their father.

Our three days together was a life-changing time for both of us.

When in doubt of my capability as a parent I read the text below, sent to me from my child during our holiday:

'I've climbed down the cliff and am just watching the ocean. I'll take a video. This is the greatest experience. Just thinking and listening to the waves in the dead of night. Thank you for taking this trip with me. I love you.'

Transform into a SWAN

My life has transformed. I have moved from love to abuse and homelessness, then to my new home and self-acceptance. I have seen the ugly side of life, and through support, writing, acceptance and nourishing my soul, I have been able to transform my life. You too can be a SWAN and transform your life.

Support: Support can come from various sources. I found support from the weight loss group when I was open about my depression. With their support I achieved my exercise goals, tracked my food intake and learnt how to cook again and my depression improved. Also pivotal to my recovery was my mental health care team which included a psychiatrist, psychologist and community mental health nurse. Ensure you have professional support. Make new and re-establish old friendships, and you will see hope. Take the time to reconnect with a loved one – the experience will be healing for you both.

Writing: Writing is a form of renewal; choose treasured retreats to spend time alone so you can write and begin to heal. Start a daily journal. Write in a way that evaluates the experience and derives meaning from the events – this is the healing element of writing. My aim is to be a published author. As you read this, I have achieved my dream. Writing has helped me heal and achieve my dream – it can help you transform, too.

Acceptance: I learnt Tara Brach's approach to radical self-acceptance. This includes practising mindfulness, self-love and self-forgiveness. I learnt the skills to reframe my shame of self-aversion and discover true refuge. By accepting ourselves for who we are, and acknowledging our most painful experiences, we begin to truly love ourselves and begin to heal ourselves. Then you will find an inner peace.

Nourish your soul: I feel nurtured by nature and neighbours. Bring nature into your life – plant a garden. In a raised garden bed I planted seeds under the shade of a rambling orange trumpet vine. I tended to the garden's needs, watched it grow and it nourished my soul. I walked, taking 'mindfulness' photos, capturing moments representing emerging confidence or anguish. I had them printed and created small photo books. I walk the local walking paths surrounded by trees. 'Good morning' greetings from my neighbours along the busy trails are part of my morning ritual. Nourish your soul by creating a ritual for being nurtured by both nature and neighbour.

© Broken to Brilliant

CHAPTER ELEVEN

LOSS, GRIEF, DESPAIR – REPAIR WITH GRATITUDE

'Even during the abyss of abuse, adversity, grief and despair, if you take the time to look, you will find something to be grateful for. Get a grip on your life through gratitude.'

FOR 45 MINUTES WITH THE SOUNDS OF CLANKING AND CLANGing in the background and the rhythmic rocking of the train, my head hung low. Large black sunglasses covered most of my face. Tears plopped onto my sunglasses, rolled down the lenses and landed in my lap. In my scrawling, illegible handwriting, I read and re-read the hardest list I have ever written: the ten things I was grateful for.

No! I am not uncaring, thankless or entitled. It was very hard to find things to be grateful for when facing so much loss. I had lost my marriage, our family home, our lives in another city, my friends, my job, my car, possessions we could not take and my income.

My children had lost their family home, their family unit, their friends, their sports, their possessions and their lives as they knew them.

We had lost our family – what society calls a successful family. There was a big, gaping hole in my heart and it hurt like hell. I felt my pain and the pain of each of my children.

We were experiencing simultaneously many of the items listed as the top ten life stressors. Abuse and violence, crime, relationship and family breakdown, loss of job, changing schools, moving to a new house, loss of friends, a change in our social supports and more.

I first wrote my list when a book I was reading on the train told me to write ten things I was grateful for in my life. I mean – really? How can you be grateful when you have lost so much? What is left to feel grateful about?

I felt so sad, so alone, so angry at the entire world. The children were feeling all these things as well. For f__'s sake, give me a break! Give us all a b___y break!

Whatever possessed me – I don't even know that I thought too much about it – my hand went into my backpack and pulled out my small spiral-bound notebook. As I flipped through the pages filled with to-do lists, how much money we had left – zero! – I found a page that had some space to write.

As the train rocked back and forth, I wrote ... 'I am grateful for my children, the people who have helped me, for the place we are staying in.'

I could not get to ten. So I had to list each person who had helped me separately, list each child, family members, our beds, the food we had, the new part-time job I had, the school that accepted the children when there were no spaces left.

Finally, there it was – scrawled, tear-stained, smudged: a list of ten things to be grateful for.

Then each day as I travelled to work, I would read my dog-eared little spiral-bound book.

That wasn't all. Another book suggested expressing gratitude before going to sleep. I obeyed – to remind myself not to wallow in the muckiness of the losses and fall asleep on a tear-soaked pillow.

I made a list on the biggest sticky notes you could find – an A3 size. I stuck two pages on the wall beside my bed. Each night before going to sleep I would read the list of what I was thankful for and say additional things I was thankful for from that day.

As soon as my feet touched the floor each morning I would read the list. As I sat on that train each day with tears streaming down my face, I would read the list. As we sat at the dinner table together my children and I would chat about what we were grateful for (of course, this did not always go well every day). Before I got into bed, I would again express thanks for all we had and all we had received that day.

I continued this practice for days, weeks, months and years. The practice of expressing gratitude changed my attitude from being angry at the world – and letting everyone I met know about it – to being more positive, grateful and joyful.

I am not suggesting that you try the practice of gratitude on my recommendation alone. In each of our books, domestic violence survivors have used the power of gratitude to help them rebuild their lives.

- 'When you find beauty in everything, including yourself,

then you have replaced hate with gratitude. Keep a gratitude journal and write everything down that you are grateful for at the end of each day. Replace hate with gratitude.' *Broken to Brilliant*, Chapter Three: Pieces to a better life

- 'I thank my family for being who they were in my life and for ultimately giving me the means to take a giant leap forward in my life. I truly honour them for that gift … Love your life lessons. Your story is not you. Look at your life events as lessons in life and have gratitude for these experiences – this will change your mindset.' *Broken to Brilliant*, Chapter Six: What badge are you wearing?
- 'Express Gratitude: Be thankful to others; show your gratitude to them – e.g. a thank you card. You never know how your appreciation can change a person's life; this small gesture can make them feel valued and appreciated and be the catalyst for them to break free.' *Broken to Brilliant*, Chapter Seven: Genuine human kindness can change your life
- 'I am very thankful for all that I have. I am thankful every day that I am fit and healthy. I am thankful for my life experiences. It has made me who I am. These experiences have enabled me to understand other people's misfortunes. I have a life filled with happiness and I am truly thankful. Thanks to Broken to Brilliant for helping me share my story. It was hard to relive it but telling it has been healing. It has also helped me reflect and feel

thankful for my happy life.' *Broken to Brilliant*, Chapter Nine: My wish for happiness
- 'Appreciation and Action: Feelings of gratitude and really connecting and appreciating what you truly have is required. At first this may not be easy to see but it takes practice. Take action, be grateful, read and re-write your list every day, morning and night.' *Broken to Brilliant*, Chapter Ten: We all need a slice of SPAM
- 'Express gratitude for what has gone well in your day.' *Terror to Triumph*, Chapter Four: Nothing changes if nothing changes
- 'We are moving forward in love, light and gratitude. Namaste.' *Terror to Triumph*, Chapter Eight: Boundaries, balance and priorities
- 'I am grateful that I: had been holding two soft small hands, as this gave me the courage to step into the fear of leaving the domestic violence situation … I had the chance to read the words from other survivors that breathed hope and inspiration into my soul … Reading to develop a new mindset, expressing gratitude for all that you have and noticing the wealth of nature.' *Terror to Triumph*, Chapter Ten: Two small hands
- 'I found gratitude for my experiences, as they've shaped who I've become. I have the power and wisdom to break the cycle of dysfunction, and the opportunity to make a difference in the world.' *Shattered to Shining*, Chapter One: The glue of self-love
- 'I opened myself up to self-development, meditation,

gratitude and so much more. I cannot begin to explain the depths of self-knowledge this has led me to, along with the exquisite healing power I have been able to experience.' *Shattered to Shining*, Chapter Three: Warrior

'Ugh!' I hear your inner voice say. 'Still not convinced.'

Well, you do not have to believe survivors' personal lived experiences. Many mentors, coaches and experts worldwide have released videos, podcasts and blogs describing the health and life benefits of practising gratitude. Also, there is plenty of researched evidence to support the expression of gratitude as a means of healing.

What is gratitude? It is defined as 'the appreciation of what is valuable and meaningful to oneself; it is a general state of thankfulness and/or appreciation' (Sansone, 2010).

It will be worth your while to visit the words of wisdom about gratitude from thought leaders around the world. These are a few:

- **Brene Brown** has undertaken 12 years of research using 11,000 pieces of data. She found that practising gratitude invites joy into our lives.
- **Tony Robbins** believes you can't be angry and grateful simultaneously, and that gratitude is the antidote to the things that mess us up.
- **Oprah Winfrey** believes the single greatest thing you can do to change your life today is to start being grateful for what you have right now, and that everyone has something to be grateful for.
- **Deepak Chopra** says gratitude is a crucial quality to

cultivate to bring more happiness, joy, and energy into your heart and life.

Research has discovered many benefits of being grateful, including ways it can improve our physical, psychological and mental wellbeing. Studies have found gratitude:

- is associated with positive thoughts, positive feelings, and positive behaviours, and these factors in turn are linked to greater wellbeing
- can improve psychological wellbeing
- lowers heart rate and blood pressure
- reduces anxiety
- reduces depression
- improves sleep quality and length of sleep
- improves feelings of joy and happiness by 15–25%
- improves relationships as you get along better with other people
- reduces feelings of loneliness and isolation.

The key to reaping the benefits of gratitude is to be consistent in practising gratitude. Just practising it for one week or so will not lead to the health benefits mentioned above. Practising gratitude needs to become a daily practice for the rest of your life. Here is a suggested daily plan:

- Morning – meditate and/or read your gratitude list.
- Each day – offer sincere thanks to people throughout each day.
- Dinner – at the evening meal share with family and/or friends what you are grateful for.

- Bedtime – before you close your eyes focus on three things that you are grateful for that day.

Some domestic violence refuges are now integrating gratitude into their programs. They are introducing the 5-minute gratitude journal as it can help shift the focus from traumatic events to being able to see what is in your life to be thankful for.

But do not be mistaken – practising gratitude doesn't mean you are happy and positive at all times. It doesn't mean you never feel other emotions like betrayal, loss, frustration and anger. You still need to feel these, though practising gratitude stops us wallowing in the deep mud of victimhood and helps us to move to living life as a survivor and thriver. Keep it real and feel.

What you can do to be more GRATEFUL

There are so many ways we can practise gratitude. What is important is to do something that works for you, that fits in with your life, and that makes you feel alive and joyful. Below is a list of actions you can choose to do to help you feel more grateful every day.

Grateful jar: Create a jar and label it 'gratitude'. Each day drop in a small note about what you are grateful for. On New Year's Day read all the things you were grateful for last year and start your year on the right note.

Ritual: If religious, pray about your gratitude. Create a family gratitude ritual. Before each meal invite each family member to share one thing they're grateful for. Listen attentively as they share and 'take in the good' from their life as well as your own.

Appreciation: Count your blessings. At the end of the day or the end of the week write down three things that you are grateful for. Download a gratitude app, journal, and/or snap photos and share what you are grateful for.

Thoughts: Practise mindfulness and meditation about what and whom you are grateful for.

Express and exercise:
- Express thanks – say thank you in a sincere and meaningful way.
- Exercise – go on a gratitude walk and appreciate and express gratitude for the world around you.

Finish each day with gratitude: Before going to sleep each night, say three things you are grateful for.

Uplifting: Take a video or photo of items around you that bring you joy and that you are grateful to have seen, for example, a beautiful flower, shells on a beach.

Letters: Write and send a letter to someone for whom you are grateful. Send short simple notes or cards of thanks. Write letters to yourself. Journal each day about things that you are grateful for.

© Broken to Brilliant

Bibliography

Allen, S. 2018. *The science of gratitude. A white paper prepared for the John Templeton Foundation*. Greater Good Science Center, Berkeley. <https://ggsc.berkeley.edu/images/uploads/GGSC-JTF_White_Paper-Gratitude-FINAL.pdf>.

Brown, B. 2018. 'Brené Brown on Joy and Gratitude'. *Global Leadership Network*, 21 November. <https://globalleadership.org/articles/leading-yourself/brene-brown-on-joy-and-gratitude/>.

Tracy, B. 2016. *The four A's for expressing gratitude*. 22 Nov. <https://youtu.be/ZLMbaNG3G3Q>.

Cheng, S-T., Tsui, P.K., & Lam, J.H.M. 2015. 'Improving mental health in health care practitioners: Randomized controlled trial of a gratitude intervention'. *Journal of Consulting and Clinical Psychology*, 83(1), 177–186. <https://www.ncbi.nlm.nih.gov/pubmed/25222798>.

Harvard Health Publishing: Harvard Medical School. 2011. 'In praise of gratitude'. *Harvard Mental Health Letter*, November (updated 5 June 2019). <https://www.health.harvard.edu/newsletter_article/in-praise-of-gratitude>.

Hellman, C.M., and Casey, G. 2017. 'Camp HOPE as an intervention for children exposed to domestic violence: A program evaluation of hope, and strength of character'. *Child and Adolescent Social Work Journal*, 34(3), 269–276. doi:10.1007/s10560-016-1460-6.

Layous, K., Sweeny, K., Armenta, C., Na, S., Choi, I., & Lyubomirsky, S. 2017. 'The proximal experience of gratitude'. *PloS One*, 12(7), e0179123. doi:10.1371/journal.pone0179123.

Miller, K. 2019. '14 Health benefits of practicing gratitude according to science'. *PositivePsychology.com*, 18 June (updated 3 July 2019). <https://positivepsychologyprogram.com/gratitude-appreciation/>.

Robbins, T. 2016. 'Tony Robbins: "Gratitude is the solution to anger and fear": "Making a difference in any measurable way grabs me". *Thrive Global*, 30 November. <https://medium.com/thrive-global/tony-robbins-gratitude-is-the-solution-to-anger-and-fear-c3fa819825c>.

Sansone, R.A., and Sansone, L.A. 2010. 'Gratitude and well being: The benefits of appreciation', *Psychiatry (Edgmont)*, 7(11), 18–22. <https://www.ncbi.nlm.nih.gov/pmc/articles/PMC3010965/>.

The Chopra Center. 2019. *Cultivate the healing power of gratitude*. <https://chopra.com/articles/cultivate-the-healing-power-of-gratitude>.

Winfrey, O. 2014. 'What you need to know about the power of gratitude'. *Oprah.com*, 21 November. <http://www.oprah.com/oprahshow/what-you-need-to-know-about-the-power-of-gratitude>.

Winfrey, O. 2011. 'What Oprah knows about the power of gratitude'. *Oprah's life class*, 28 October. <http://www.oprah.com/oprahs-lifeclass/what-oprah-knows-about-the-power-of-gratitude-video>.

Wood, A.M., Joseph, S., Lloyd, J., & Atkins, S. 2009. 'Gratitude influences sleep through the mechanism of pre-sleep cognitions'. *Journal of Psychosomatic Research*, 66(1), 43–48. <http://citeseerx.ist.psu.edu/viewdoc/download?doi=10.1.1.324.4175&rep=rep1&type=pdf>.

CHAPTER TWELVE

THE IMPACT OF WRITING MY STORY

SEVERAL AUTHORS FROM OUR PREVIOUS BOOKS *BROKEN TO Brilliant* and *Terror to Triumph* share how the experience has changed their lives.

Unlocking the 'Aliveness'

> *'The authors' collective souls have risen out of the burning embers and ashes, to form a bright and shining light – sending the power of our stories far and wide.'*

Seeing the words all laid out on the pages of my chapter was both thrilling and terrifying. It doesn't seem to matter how many times I re-read my story – the tears just keep flowing.

I guess there were many times in my life I was not able to express them, so now when I touch those places of sadness, a river of tears flows forth. The fact that I am able to express such strong emotions, and hold space for them to be welcomed and comforted, in a way I had never been able to do before, is in itself a real sign of healing.

My old habits of shutting off or avoiding strong emotions

like sadness, fear, anger and even love are finally also losing their stranglehold on my ability to feel alive.

Thinking back, I have this vision of pulling my dying, damaged body out of the murky, black quicksand and looking at it, lying pale and lifeless. Was it possible to bring it back to life? Not just to live a hollow existence as an empty shell, but to reignite fire and passion? To have every cell in my body electrified and ALIVE?

'Yes' was the whisper – and the transformation began.

An essential part of that transformation is finally feeling in every nerve of my body a sense of safety and belonging. This has become so much sharper and more prominent with the connections forged through writing my story for *Terror to Triumph*. It's as if the authors' collective souls have risen out of the ashes of the burning embers, drawing together to form a bright and shining light sending the power of our stories far and wide.

Writing my story and sharing it with the world as part of the book has been for me a profoundly healing experience. It was not only about what happened but, more importantly, about how I have gone on to shine. My voice continues to echo louder and louder as I build confidence and draw support from those who surround me.

There has been a huge shift for me as now I know I am not only strong enough to save myself and my children, I am strong enough to reach out and support others to heal and grow.

This has been no easy feat. I had to do a lot of hard work and make personal sacrifices to get to this point. Yet it has been incredibly worth it. I have turned my world around from hiding and avoiding triggers that haunted my every moment, to a life filled with glimmers that allow me to shine, and a deep sense of safety and peace.

A vital key to this has been learning how to reconnect with the world and the people in it. For someone who was abused and isolated for so long, and suffered so much at the hands of those who loved them, reconnecting was almost incomprehensible. Yet it is an essential part of the human hardwire, and something I deeply yearned for.

Connections forged in a world co-created by sharing our terrors and triumphs have ignited my sense of aliveness. It is infectious, this sense of being alive – really alive. For all those who stood beside me as I gazed down at the lifeless body beside the quicksand, thank you for not giving up on me as I do the same for you now.

I am beside you. I see you. I feel you. Together we are reaching through the power of our past.

You can transform your life by saying yes to life and being alive. I said YES, and you can as well.

Yes: Say yes to living, say yes to moving forward, to wanting more in your life. Allow your yearning for more to drive you forward.

Express emotions: Allow yourself the space to be able to express strong emotions, and hold space for them. Welcome their release and be comforted that you are able to do this now – it is a sign of healing.

Support, and shared stories: Saying yes to sharing my story in *Terror to Triumph* allowed me to find the support I needed;

it created a sense of belonging. Through our shared stories our souls connected – I felt I belonged and was safe.

A special breed: survivors

Being asked to write my story in the book *Terror to Triumph* was probably one of my greatest honours and also one of my greatest tests, mentally and emotionally. Writing brought peace that my story would finally be told, but also fear. Hours and sometimes days spent pondering.

Some days the words would flow – I knew what I wanted to talk about. My hand would ache, I was writing so fast. Some days were spent just looking at a blank page.

Looking for words that were strangers now, worried about what the reader would think, the unexpected nightmares, sleepless nights and flashbacks that held me back, reliving over and over again. All of a sudden a word would come back to me, bringing joy.

Being a newly-formed author allowed me to be true to myself, to discover what really was left of me after the abuse, and to discover more about my own recovery. Learning to finally let go of the past. Returning the drama that was given to me to its rightful owner, my abuser. Meeting and making new friends with fellow survivors who had stories that only we could understand. Beginning again that moral inventory of achievements that were denied so long ago.

My anxiety and stress levels were high on book release day. Getting ready was a slow fumble, my speech unpractised. Sitting in the back seat of the car trying to find the brake pedal for my racing mind.

But all of this was soon gone when I opened that door to see – for the first time – our books, on a table decorated with white flowers. Smiling faces that I remembered from this journey. The sounds of laughter. The great weight of anticipation left as I was greeted. My smile returned. I was finally home, and the world could read my story that was so different from the one my abuser told.

I took extra copies that I signed with words of wisdom I have learnt on my journey, for those who are beginning their journey in confusion. One went to my local library where they witnessed me in my struggle. One went to my doctor who could now learn the truth. One to the police station that turned me away when I asked for help. Another to my neuropsychologist who helped me understand what's happened to me during dismantlement and taught me skills in recovery. He helped me find my voice, and for that I will be eternally grateful. Another to a stranger I met by chance at a New Year's party – who was beginning his journey as a survivor where recovery had no meaning. Others to my friends who witnessed my struggle, to help them understand a survivor's journey.

One person refused to read my story – my mother. But I'm okay with that now. Years of trying to find help were cast aside. The child she had brought up was an unrecognisable stranger now – the words I spoke were an embarrassment.

Helping other men and women that are going through domestic violence is a part of my everyday now. I have learnt so many skills that I need to pass on and that are so desperately required. I can see it in their faces – not understanding the word 'recovery' or completely unaware of their own mental illness as a victim of domestic violence.

I share my story, not only in social media recovery groups but also in person – which has led me to setting up a charity called S.O.S. (Shame Of Silence) for male victims of domestic violence. For that I must thank those who have supported me, and the team at Broken to Brilliant that offer endless help, support and encouragement, and who allowed me to help the authors of the next book on their journey – and for that I am eternally grateful.

You see, we authors are a special breed – we survived.

Free to shine

When I wrote my chapter in *Broken to Brilliant*, I didn't feel strong enough to tell the story of the day I decided I was done. But now I do. Telling my story has changed me.

***

The stars are shining brighter and brighter in front of my eyes … but it is half past ten in the morning. It isn't night-time, but it is getting darker!

I can feel myself slipping into that delicious transition to sleep. But I am not in my bed – I am slipping into unconsciousness. He has his hands around my throat again!

Instinctively, I know he isn't going to stop this time. My body is getting really floppy and my legs are buckling underneath me.

Suddenly, I see a vision of my children living alone with him;

the protective Mother inside me starts to rise. I will NOT let this continue. This time he is definitely NOT going to stop the choking! Quick! F___ing do something before he kills you, and the boys are left alone with him! Is that what you want?

What did that police officer tell us to do back when I was 19? Quick! Think! Oh yeah ... head butt!

I continue to physically fight back because I've made up my mind this time – today is the day. I've had enough. He is so wrong for how he is choosing to treat me with his 'communication'.

'What you are doing to me is against the law. It's called domestic violence and I've had enough. I'm calling the police.' My throat is stinging, my voice gravelly from the damage he has done, as I reach for the phone.

This is not love. This is not a safe or respectful marriage. It hasn't been for years. I just don't have any more forgiveness to give. I want better for my children. I'd like better for me.

If he can do this to me, he could do it to my children. Now they are four and five years old, it's only a matter of time. He says my eldest looks just like me and knows how to push his buttons. What the hell does that even mean! Does that mean my children deserve to have the living s___ choked out of them whenever they anger their father? I will not let that happen. I never want my children to experience this terror. I'm so shattered trying to live this life.

That was 15 years ago.

He followed through and did exactly what he always said he'd do if we split up.

He tried to grab everything I held dear, including my children and my sanity. Like so many other mothers, I was dragged through the courts for many years even though I offered to go 50/50 in dividing the assets.

Today, neither of my children wants anything to do with their father. They don't have any respect for him, only hatred. They both live for the day that he no longer paces this earth. They still carry emotional wounds from the damage he caused to their little developing personalities.

Back then the family court **made** them go on access visits. They were nine years old when they decided they no longer felt safe to visit him. I had to go back to court for their little voices to be heard. Child protection is **everyone's business,** yet it was only me that stood up and spoke for them to be heard.

I'm here. I'm alive. I'm flipping proud of the woman and mother that I am. I can look in the mirror once more and smile with pride at the reflection I see.

Every time I am asked to gently educate about domestic violence (or domestic terror as it should be called), it never matters if it's to 20 in a classroom or 700 at a White Ribbon Day launch, the feedback is always overwhelmingly positive and leads to positive change, so I keep doing it while I have the authentic energy to do it.

I can be myself and can enjoy making others giggle with my kooky sense of humour. I've even had a go at stand-up comedy and made everyone laugh! I'm an author in our first book *Broken to Brilliant*. I wrote the foreword in our second book *Terror to Triumph*, and here I am again in our third book. And there will be many more books for new authors to tell their stories of survival to inspire others to reach their successes.

I am financially independent. I have finally bought a home in the suburb of my choice. I drive a 4WD and can go anywhere in it – I'm about to drive to Uluru with another author and celebrate our survival and thriving. I have excelled in my career and have surrounded myself with safe and respectful relationships. I say, 'No, thank you,' when I want to and let unsafe and disrespectful relationships go when I need to.

I am grateful for developing my new gratitude motto of FACC:

- **Freedom**: to do what I want
- **Ability**: to always try
- **Choices**: in every aspect of my life
- **Confidence**: to always have a go.

I look to my future with pride, optimism and gratitude. I can be exactly who I want to be. I can fail when I need to and learn from it.

I can smile with pride at the Warrior/Girl/Woman/Mother/Sister/Daughter/Friend in the mirror.

If I met me, I'd want to hang out with me and be my best friend. How many of us can honestly say that?

That was then, this is now

I used to take comfort from the words, 'Wow! You are so strong!' or, 'You are one of the toughest people I know.' But are these really compliments? Is this how people see me? How did I end up like that?

These are the questions I have asked myself since writing my story in *Broken to Brilliant*.

I was surprised that anybody resonated with my story, as I had never thought of myself or what I achieved as of value to anyone else. But I have been pleased some people could relate to it and, if it helps one person, the ripple effect could help generations to come.

When writing my story I realised just what I had achieved – as most people would if they condensed several years of their life to a few thousand words. I had managed to pay off my house and had no mortgage. I had an investment property. My children and I had been on overseas holidays. They had gone to private high schools and, now grown, are doing well in their own businesses.

But is that really what being 'brilliant' is all about? In some ways, maybe.

But writing my story also made me think about what I had to do and become to achieve those goals. I am proud of the achievement. But was I pushing to prove to 'him' and others that he hadn't broken me, that I could do it all on my own and didn't need anyone? Had I become too tough?

One thing I do know is, after the break-up, I felt a massive responsibility to just stay alive. Who would take care of and love my children as I did? Who would give them the good life I had planned for them? I needed to live a long life, so I'd better harden up.

The years after I was out of the domestic abuse situation and finally settled were really happy. I enjoyed rearing my children, seeing them develop into smart, caring, achieving adults. There were the usual ups and downs, but that's just life.

However, being on my own now that the children have moved out, I can see that writing my story brought finalisation. For such a long time, I was trying so hard to do everything that I never stopped to realise it was over. That part of my life which happened over 20 years ago is no longer my story.

It made me realise that, while strength and toughness are okay, I don't need to be strong and tough all the time. I do not need to continually be in defence mode, pushing hard to make sure I never go back into a situation like that again. I don't need to prove to anyone that I can do everything, and it is okay to soften and trust a little more.

I possibly have 30-plus years of life still to live. I want to make it count. I plan on going back to study – because I believe lifelong learning is important, but also it is good for me mentally and physically. I plan on staying at my job as I have no real desire to retire fully. I will also continue to work with the charity Broken to Brilliant as I enjoy seeing fellow domestic violence survivors thrive. I will spend as much time as I can with my children and friends, as they are my world.

So, my new acronym is **NEW HOME:**
- **N**ever stop setting goals
- **E**ducation – lifelong
- **W**ork at a job you like
- **H**elp others
- **O**ld and new friends – love them
- **M**ental and physical health is important

- Enjoy life.

Writing my story finally made me see I am safe – both physically and emotionally – because that was then, this is now, and I am free to be me.

Step into the arena – be vulnerable, brave, resilient and brilliant

When I first left the crazy, confusing life of abuse, I wanted to write and share what went on behind the white picket fake-fence that I painted for so long. Now I am glad the rebuilding of life got in the way of revealing that early writing to the world.

During the labour of rebuilding – wait, you need to get an understanding of the effort needed for rebuilding. Think about building a house with mud bricks. Those bricks are made by you working through the thick mud of emotions. You have to make each and every brick first.

Then you need to wait until those emotional bricks harden. During the hardening, you must learn how to build the walls and a roof while keeping yourself together, presentable and sociable.

The brick drying time was very valuable, because I learnt so much. It allowed me to move through the cycle of loss and grief. The depth of despair and gushing waterfalls of tears. Through the angry-at-the-entire-world phase. Yes, angry at everyone who helped to keep me there. Angry at every person and system that hindered us getting out.

Time – I needed the time – plus the mountains of education. I was changing and learning as I inhaled information to help me understand what had happened to me and my children.

When I shared my first story, who would have thought that I could have turned all that adversity into a positive. Sharing my story took me places I never dreamed of venturing. The bright lights and red carpet of Hollywood, rubbing shoulders with Jack Canfield. Yes! That's correct, the author of the *Chicken Soup for the Soul* series.

This was the gift of confidence I needed. Yes, my story was valued and real. I could write. I had changed, I had a different attitude. I was grateful for all that I had and all the support I received.

My dream had been evolving to help survivors move forward and share their story of recovery after abuse. Two years later the collective of Broken to Brilliant was born, breathing support and kindness into survivors' lives.

Since sharing my story in *Broken to Brilliant*, I thought that maybe I had done all the tweaking of my life that I needed to do. I had shared my story; it was out there. I had done so much education and work on myself – surely I did not need more?

But life happens, and there are so many ups and downs. Some of those are normal life events we all deal with like big birthdays and the empty nest. Other stumbles are directly attributed to the post-trauma of abuse. Those unsuspecting triggers that take you back to the anxiety. The surging adrenalin and my fists are up – I am in full fight. Fists and words flying – defending my honour, my truth, my earnest efforts. Or the tears dripping uncontrollably down my face as a health professional attempts to help me with neck pain. All I can think is I might die, as they lay their hands on my neck for a therapeutic manipulation.

Rebuilding life after abuse, is not a 'get out and you are suddenly okay' process. It is a long-term recovery, with a lot of lessons, and a lot of tweaks needed to yourself and your life to keep you moving forward. I thought I had opened myself and let my story out. But in the words of Brené Brown, I had not truly stepped into the arena and been truly vulnerable. Really? Yes, really.

This year, I took sharing my story to another level. How could there be another level of sharing? I learnt that there was. For domestic violence month, I stepped forward trembling, scared, nervous, embarrassed and ashamed. I stood in front of a room full of my work colleagues in the arena of vulnerability and courage, telling them about my dirty laundry.

If that was not enough, the word, 'Yes!' came out of my mouth again. 'Yes, I will volunteer to be in a video to promote domestic violence month to the whole organisation.' As filming was occurring, unplanned, personal words escaped my lips. I could not breathe them back in. Filming stopped. I asked, 'Did I really just say that I was a domestic violence survivor?'

'Yes, you did, thank you for sharing.'

After the video was released, I walked past the desk of a colleague. He said, 'I saw the video. Thank you.' That was a relief. I have not watched the video. Yes, I know there is another lesson or tweak to be made before I will be able to watch that video.

Sharing my story has taken me from a few thousand words on a page to the red carpet. But the brightest of lights are my pride for my children, working with fellow survivors – now friends, establishing a charity, running narrative therapy workshops and gratitude walks, helping others move through the mud to rebuild their lives. Paying it forward. I am grateful for all that I have in my life and that our work has benefited so many survivors.

Step into the arena with us – be vulnerable, brave, resilient and brilliant.

Our tribe of survivors can now smile as we continue to make tweaks and travel our life journey ahead.

- **Triggers:** Triggers can catch you unexpectedly – it's okay to not be okay, but do not wallow. Learn what your triggers are and catch them early. Replace with a positive experience.
- **Writing:** Writing about your experience can be therapeutic, though the focus of your writing needs to be on how far you have come and express gratitude.
- **Education and exercise:** It will take lots of self-education and physical exercise to help you move into the new chapter of life.
- **Attitude of gratitude:** To develop an attitude of gratitude, express thankfulness for things in your life. Start with the simple things, such as the sound of the birds singing, that you woke up today, that you are reading this book.
- **Kindness:** Being kind requires courage and strength. Be kind to yourself and others. Practise kindness every day.
- **Support:** You cannot do this alone. You need support – find your tribe.

GLOSSARY

THE PEOPLE IN THIS BOOK HAVE EXPERIENCED MANY FORMS OF ongoing abuse. This glossary provides definitions for domestic and family violence and the associated behaviours.

Domestic and family violence, also known as domestic violence, family violence, partner violence or intimate partner violence, is a pattern of abusive behaviour between family members and/or intimate partners, usually, though not exclusively, taking place in the home, that over time puts one person in a position of power over another, and causes fear. It is often referred to as a pattern of coercion and control. Abusers are sometimes called 'perpetrators of violence'.[36][37][38][39]

Family and domestic violence is any violent, threatening, coercive or controlling behaviour that occurs in current or past family, domestic or intimate relationships. This includes not only physical injury but direct or indirect threats, sexual assault, emotional and psychological torment, economic control, damage to property, social isolation and any behaviour which causes a person to live in fear or torment.

Types of abusive behaviour associated with domestic and family violence include:
- **Physical abuse** – including direct assaults on the body (shaking, slapping, pushing), use of weapons, driving dangerously, destruction of property, abuse of pets in front

of family members, assault of children, locking the victim out of the house, and sleep deprivation.

- **Sexual abuse** – any form of forced sex or sexual degradation, such as sexual activity without consent, causing pain during sex, assaulting genitals, coercive sex without protection against pregnancy or sexually transmitted disease, making the victim perform sexual acts unwillingly, criticising, or using sexually degrading insults.
- **Emotional abuse** – blaming the victim for all problems in the relationship, constantly comparing the victim with others to undermine self-esteem and self-worth, sporadic sulking, withdrawing all interest and engagement (e.g. weeks of silence), blackmail. Domestic violence threats are a form of emotional abuse and are threats made within the context of an abusive relationship. Whether the threats are of a physical, sexual or emotional nature, they are all designed to further control the victim by instilling fear and ensuring compliance.
- **Verbal abuse** – continual 'put downs' and humiliation, either privately or publicly, with attacks following clear themes that focus on intelligence, sexuality, body image and capacity as a parent and spouse or capable person.
- **Social abuse** – systematic isolation from family and friends through techniques such as ongoing rudeness to family and friends, moving to locations where the victim knows nobody, and forbidding or physically preventing the victim from going out and meeting people.
- **Economic abuse** – complete control of all monies, no access

to bank accounts, providing only an inadequate 'allowance', using any wages earned by the victim for household expenses.
- **Spiritual abuse** – denying access to ceremonies, land or family, preventing religious observance, forcing victims to do things against their beliefs, denigration of cultural background, or using religious teachings or cultural tradition as a reason for violence.

The above behaviours are from Tually S, Faulkner D, Cutler C and Slatter M. 2008. "Women, Domestic and Family Violence and Homelessness: A Synthesis Report." Office for Women and Inspire Foundation. Flinders Institute for Housing, Urban and Regional Research Flinders University

<https://www.dss.gov.au/sites/default/files/documents/05_2012/synthesis_report2008.pdf>

CONTACT NUMBERS

Australia National
- 1800 RESPECT (1800 737 732): 24 hour national sexual assault, family & domestic violence counselling line for any Australian who has experienced, or is at risk of, family and domestic violence and/or sexual assault
- Lifeline 131 114: National number who can help put you in contact with a crisis service in your state (24 hours)
- Police or Ambulance 000: In an emergency for police or ambulance
- Translating and Interpreting Service 131 450: Phone to gain access to an interpreter in your own language (free)
- Mensline Australia 1300 789 978: Supports men and boys who are dealing with family and relationship difficulties
- Kids Help Line 1800 551 800: Telephone counselling for children and young people. Email and web counselling: www.kidshelp.com.au
- Australian Childhood Foundation 1800 381 581: Counselling for children and young people affected by abuse www.childhood.org.au
- Relationships Australia 1300 364 277: Support groups and counselling on relationships, and for abusive and abused partners. Website: www.relationships.com.au

- Blue Knot Foundation (Adults Surviving Child Abuse) 1300 657 380: A service to adult survivors, their friends and family and the health care professionals who support them. Support line: www.asca.org.au
- National Disability Abuse and Neglect Hotline 1800 880 052: An Australia-wide telephone hotline for reporting abuse and neglect of people with disability. www.disabilityhotline.org
- LGBTIQ Domestic Violence Information: Another Closet www.anothercloset.com.au
- LGBTIQ Qlife 1800 184 527
- Transgender and Transsexual People: Gender Centre (02) 9569 2366: Services for people with gender issues. www.gendercentre.org.au
- National Suicide Prevention – Lifeline 13 11 14

Australian Capital Territory
- Domestic Violence Crisis Service 02 6280 0900
- Rape Crisis Centre (24 Hours) 02 6247 2525
- Canberra Men's Centre 02 6230 6999
- Legal Aid ACT 1300 654 314
- Women's Legal Service 02 6257 4499

New South Wales
- Domestic Violence Line 1800 656 463 / 1800 671 442 TTY (Hearing impaired)
- Rape Crisis Service 1800 424 017 / 02 9181 4349 TTY
- Immigrant Women's Speakout Association 02 9635 8022
- Interrelate Family Centres 1300 473 528

- Legal Aid NSW 1300 888 529

Northern Territory
- Domestic Violence Crisis Line 1800 737 732
- Domestic & Family Violence Centre (YWCA) 08 8932 9155
- Sexual Assault Referral Centre 08 8922 6472
- Men's Line 1300 789 978
- Northern Territory Legal Aid Commission 1800 019 343

Queensland
- Domestic Violence Telephone Service 1800 811 811 / 1800 812 225 TTY
- Sexual Assault Help Line 1800 010 120
- Men's Info Line 1800 600 636
- DV Connect Men's Line 1800 600 626
- Migrant Women's Support Service 07 3846 3490
- Legal Aid Queensland 1300 651 188
- Women's Legal Service 1800 957 957

South Australia
- Domestic Violence Crisis Line 1300 782 200
- Yarrow Place Sexual Assault Service 08 8226 8777
- Legal Service Commission 1300 366 424
- Men's Line Australia 1300 789 978
- Migrant Women's Support Services 08 8346 9417
- Women's Legal Service 08 8221 5553

Tasmania
- Family Violence Counselling and Support Service 1800 608 122
- Men's Line Australia 1300 789 978
- Sexual Assault Support Service 03 6231 1817/ 03 6334 2740
- Women's Legal Service 1800 682 468
- Legal Aid Tasmania 1300 366 611

Victoria
- Safe steps Family Violence Response Centre 1800 015 188 or 02 9322 3555
- Sexual Assault Crisis Line 1800 806 292
- Men's Referral Service 1800 065 973
- Victoria Legal Aid 1300 792 387
- Women's Legal Service 1800 682 468

Western Australia
- Women's Domestic Violence Helpline 08 9223 1188/ 1800 007 339
- Crisis Care 1800 199 008 or 9233 1111
- Sexual Assault Resource Centre 08 6458 1828 or 1800 199 888
- Men's Helpline 08 9223 1199 or 1800 000 599
- Legal Aid WA 1300 650 579
- Community Legal Centre 08 9221 9322
- Women's Legal Centre Western Australia (WLCWA) (08) 9272 8800

United States of America
- The National Domestic Violence Hotline 1-800-799-7233 | 1-800-787-3224 (TTY)

United Kingdom
- National Domestic Helpline 0808 2000 247: 24-hour National Domestic Violence Freephone Helpline

Ireland
- 24 Hour Domestic & Sexual Violence Helpline 0808 802 1414
- Email 24hrsupport@dvhelpline.org
- Text 'support' to 07797 805 839

Europe
- Women Against Violence Europe list of national phone numbers for 46 countries https://ec.europa.eu/justice/saynostopvaw/helpline.html
- Or the Helplines in Europe List https://www.coe.int/en/web/istanbul-convention/help-lines

China
- Domestic violence Hotline "Dial 110"

New Zealand Helplines
- Domestic Violence Crisis Line - 303 3939
- For more helplines https://sps.org.au/people-support/Helplines

Contact details were correct at the time of publication.

ENDNOTES

1   Anderson, K. M., & Hiersteiner, C. 2008. 'Recovering from childhood sexual abuse: Is a "storybook ending" possible?' *American Journal of Family Therapy*, 36(5), 413–424.

2   Kosenko, K., & Laboy, J. 2014. '"I survived": The content and forms of survival narratives.' *Journal of Loss and Trauma*, 19(6), 497–513. doi:10.1080/15325024.2013.808948.

3   Méndez-Negrete, J. 2013. 'Expressive creativity: Narrative text and creative cultural expressions as a healing praxis.' *Journal of Creativity in Mental Health*, 8(3), 314. doi:10.1080/15401383.2013.821934.

4   Anderson, K. M., Renner, L. M., & Danis, F. S. 2012. 'Recovery: Resilience and growth in the aftermath of domestic violence.' *Violence Against Women*, 18(11), 1279–1299.

5   Tually, S., Faulkner, D., Cutler. C., & Slatter, M. 2008. *Women, domestic and family violence and homelessness: A synthesis report*. Flinders University, Flinders Institute for Housing, Urban and Regional Research. <https://www.dss.gov.au/sites/default/files/documents/05_2012/synthesis_report2008.pdf>

6   Victorian Government, Department of Human Services. 2007. *Family violence risk assessment and risk management framework*. p. 21. <https://providers.dhhs.vic.gov.au/family-violence-risk-assessment-and-risk-management-framework>

7   The National Council to Reduce Violence against Women and their Children (NCRVWC). 2009. *Background paper to Time for Action: The National Council's plan to reduce violence against women and children,*

2009–2021. p. 13. <https://www.dss.gov.au/our-responsibilities/women/publications-articles/reducing-violence/national-plan-to-reduce-violence-against-women-and-their-children/background-paper-to-time-for-action-the-national-councils-plan-for-australia-to-reduce-violence-against-women-and-their?HTML>.

8   Evans, D. I. 2007. *Battle-scars:Long-term effects of prior domestic violence*. Centre for Women's Studies and Gender Research, Melbourne.

9   The National Council to Reduce Violence against Women and their Children (NCRVWC). 2009. *Background paper to Time for Action: The National Council's plan to reduce violence against women and children, 2009–2021*. <https://www.dss.gov.au/our-responsibilities/women/publications-articles/reducing-violence/national-plan-to-reduce-violence-against-women-and-their-children/background-paper-to-time-for-action-the-national-councils-plan-for-australia-to-reduce-violence-against-women-and-their?HTML>.

10   White Ribbon. 2019. *Signs of an abusive relationship*. <https://www.whiteribbon.org.au/understand-domestic-violence/what-is-domestic-violence/signs-abusive-relationship/>.

11   New Hope for Women. 2019. *Red flags for domestic abuse*. <http://www.newhopeforwomen.org/red-flags-for-domestic-abuse>.

12   Ali, P., McGarry, J., & Dhingra, K. 2016. 'Identifying signs of intimate partner violence.' *Emergency Nurse*, 23(9), 25–29. doi: https://doi.org/10.7748/en.23.9.25.s25.

13   Cleveland Clinic. 2018. *Domestic abuse: How to spot relationship red flags*, 7 June. <https://health.clevelandclinic.org/domestic-abuse-how-to-spot-relationship-red-flags/>.

14   Women's Domestic Violence Court Advocacy Program (WDVCAP). 2017. *Charmed and Dangerous*. Legal Aid, NSW.

<http://lacextra.legalaid.nsw.gov.au/PublicationsResourcesService/PublicationImprints/Files/754.pdf>.

15   National Coalition Against Domestic Violence. n.d. *Domestic Violence, Factsheet.* <https://www.speakcdn.com/assets/2497/domestic_violence2.pdf>.

16   Office for National Statistics. 2018. *Domestic abuse: Findings from the Crime Survey for England and Wales: Year ending March 2018.* <https://www.ons.gov.uk/peoplepopulationandcommunity/crimeandjustice/articles/domesticabusefindingsfromthecrimesurveyforenglandandwales/yearendingmarch2018>.

17   European Parliament. 2018. *Violence against women in the EU: State of play. Briefing.* <http://www.europarl.europa.eu/RegData/etudes/BRIE/2018/630296/EPRS_BRI(2018)630296_EN.pdf>.

18   DRH Lindersvold. 2019. *Violence against women in Africa 2019.* <https://oneworldcenter.eu/violence-against-women-in-africa/>.

19   Stallard, J. 2018. 'The dark reality of Russia's domestic violence laws.' *BBC*, 1 February. <https://www.bbc.co.uk/bbcthree/article/0dd0ab91-145a-4137-bf87-28d0498c8d56>.

20   Spring, M. 2018. 'Decriminalisation of domestic violence in Russia leads to fall in reported cases.' *The Guardian*, 16 August. <https://www.theguardian.com/world/2018/aug/16/decriminalisation-of-domestic-violence-in-russia-leads-to-fall-in-reported-cases>.

21   Asian Pacific Institute on Gender Based Violence. 2015. *Domestic violence, Factsheet.* <https://www.api-gbv.org/about-gbv/types-of-gbv/domestic-violence/>.

22   Australian Institute of Health and Welfare. 2019. *Family, domestic and sexual violence in Australia: continuing the national story 2019* Cat. no. FDV 3. Canberra: AIHW <https://www.aihw.gov.au/reports/

domestic-violence/family-domestic-sexual-violence-australia-2019/contents/table-of-contents>.

23   Franzway, S., Wendt, S., Moulding, N., Zufferey, C., Chung, D., & Elder, A. 2015. *Gendered violence and citizenship: The complex effects of intimate partner violence on mental health, housing and employment.* University of South Australia, Magill. <http://www.unisa.edu.au/PageFiles/71190/Gendered-Violence-and-Citizenship-report.pdf>.

24   Loxton, D., Dolja-Gore, X., Anderson, A.E., & Townsend, N. 2017. 'Intimate partner violence adversely impacts health over 16 years and across generations: A longitudinal cohort study.' *PLoS ONE*, 12(6): e0178138. <https://journals.plos.org/plosone/article/file?id=10.1371/journal.pone.0178138&type=printable>.

25   Anderson, K.M., Renner, L.M., & Danis, F.S. 2012. 'Recovery: Resilience and growth in the aftermath of domestic violence.' *Violence Against Women*, 18(11), 1279–1299.

26   Jones, A., & Vetere, A. 2017. '"You just deal with it. You have to when you've got a child": A narrative analysis of mothers' accounts of how they coped, both during an abusive relationship and after leaving.' *Clinical Child Psychology and Psychiatry*, 22(1), 74–89.

27   Parkin, S. J. 2017. *Survival after violence: The post-separation journey of women who have experienced intimate partner violence.* <https://ro.ecu.edu.au/theses/2001>.

28   Noviyanti, L.K., Hamid, A.Y.S., & Daulima, N.H.C. 2019. 'Experience of domestic violence survivor women in searching their life purpose and self-resilience.' *Journal of International Dental & Medical Research*, 12(1), p. 299, viewed 8 June 2019. <https://search.ebscohost.com/login.aspx?direct=true&AuthType=athens&db=edo&AN=135783798&site=eds-live>.

29   The National Council to Reduce Violence against Women and their Children (NCRVWC). 2009. *Background paper to Time for Action: The National Council's plan to reduce violence against women and children, 2009–2021*. p. 13. <https://www.dss.gov.au/our-responsibilities/women/publications-articles/reducing-violence/national-plan-to-reduce-violence-against-women-and-their-children/background-paper-to-time-for-action-the-national-councils-plan-for-australia-to-reduce-violence-against-women-and-their?HTML>; Department for Planning and Community Development. 2007. *Family violence risk assessment and risk management framework*, Victorian Government, Melbourne, p. 21, viewed 19 September 2011. <http://www.dhs.vic.gov.au/__data/assets/pdf_file/0006/581757/risk-assessment-risk-management-framework-2007.pdf>.

30   Trauma Recovery. 2013. *Phases of Trauma Recovery*. <https://trauma-recovery.ca/recovery/phases-of-trauma-recovery/>.

31   Community Care Division. 2004. *Women's journey away from family violence – Framework and summary*. Victorian Government Department to Human Services, Melbourne. <https://www.secasa.com.au/assets/Documents/women-s-journey-away-from-family-violence.pdf>.

32   Moore, T. 1992. *Care of the soul: a guide for cultivating depth and sacredness in everyday life*, Harper Perennial, New York.

33   Levine, B. 2012. *Beating Bipolar: How one therapist tackled his illness ... and how what he learned could help you*. Hay House, California.

34   Beyond Blue Support Service 2019, 'Types of Anxiety', *Beyond Blue Limited, Australia*, viewed 22 April 2019, < https://www.beyondblue.org.au/the-facts/anxiety/types-of-anxiety/ptsd >.

35   Brach, T. 2003. *Radical acceptance: awakening the love that heals the fear and shame within us*, Rider, London. Brach, T. 2013. *True refuge:*

Finding peace and freedom in your own awakened heart. Bantam Books, New York. Plus audiobooks of the same name.

36   World Health Organization. 2002. *World report on violence and health: Summary.* World Health Organization: Geneva. Retrieved from: <http://www.who.int/violence_injury_prevention/violence/world_report/en/summary_en.pdf>.

37   Women's Council for Domestic and Family Violence Services. 2011. *What is Domestic and Family Violence?* Retrieved from: <http://www.womenscouncil.com.au/what-is-domestic--family-violence.html>.

38   State Government of Victoria, Department of Health & Human Services. 2011. *What is family violence?* Retrieved from: <https://services.dhhs.vic.gov.au/what-family-violence>.

39   Tually S., Faulkner D., Cutler C., & Slatter, M. 2008. *Women, domestic and family violence and homelessness: A synthesis report.* Flinders Institute for Housing, Urban and Regional Research: Adelaide, SA. Retrieved from: <https://www.dss.gov.au/sites/default/files/documents/05_2012/synthesis_report2008.pdf>.

ALSO IN THIS SERIES

Broken to Brilliant
Breaking Free to be You After Domestic Violence – Stories of Strength and Success

ISBN: 978-0-9945714-0-3

'That would never happen to me. I'm too strong. I would walk out.' Those were KC Andrews' thoughts as a trainee nurse listening to a lecture on domestic violence. But when it happened to her, it took years to finally leave.

She has now rebuilt her life from the ashes of a brutal marriage, and along the way met other women who have survived the fog of fear and feelings of worthlessness – and then on the outside, endured the disbelief and bureaucratic bungles of those who should have helped.

But now, each woman's brilliance is emerging once again.

Each one tells her unique story to help readers understand the many different shapes domestic violence can take. And yet, the focus of this book is not on the horror, but the healing. Each woman shares the skills, techniques and attitudes that helped her to shine once again.

This book is for anyone who is living in an abusive relationship, knows someone who is, or has emerged and is looking for a roadmap out of darkness into the light of new beginnings.

Bronze medallist, eLit Book Awards 2017

Broken to Brilliant is an Australian not-for-profit charity where domestic violence survivors mentor other survivors to re-establish successful lives. These courageous women are mothers, accountants, nurses, managers, models, executive managers, sales trainers and account executives. Each at a different stage in re-establishment and recovery, they have banded together to share how they have rebuilt their lives.

ALSO IN THIS SERIES

Terror to Triumph
Rebuilding Your Life After Domestic Violence – Stories of Strength and Success

ISBN: 978-0-9945714-9-6

'People congratulated me when I left my abusive marriage, but I didn't feel like celebrating. I felt loss, grief, shame, anger, resentment, regret, uncertainty, relief and excitement. How can one person feel so many emotions at once? Where could I go for help? Who would understand?'

From these questions, the charity Broken to Brilliant was born, where survivors help other survivors rebuild their lives using the power of story.

In **Terror to Triumph**, twelve domestic violence survivors describe the terror they experienced and the additional challenges they encountered from a system that was supposed to help them.

Most importantly, they tell of the practical steps they have taken – physically, emotionally, psychologically and spiritually – to journey from darkness to light and build new lives. They tell of continued recovery, and how they have reclaimed their lives to reach a sense of triumph.

Broken to Brilliant is an Australian not-for-profit charity where domestic violence survivors mentor other survivors to re-establish successful lives.

When we saw the impact our first book, *Broken to Brilliant*, had on people's lives – how the words breathed hope into people's hearts, how it gave them a spark that jump-started a new chapter in their lives, and how the power of people's stories created ripples of recovery and repair – we could not turn away and stop these ripples of healing. There had to be a second book.

We salute each of our authors for their courage and dedication, and hope *Terror to Triumph* will bring change and possibility into your life, too.

www.ingramcontent.com/pod-product-compliance
Lightning Source LLC
Chambersburg PA
CBHW070544010526
44118CB00012B/1215